SOLD TO THE HIGHEST BIDDER

SOLD TO THE HIGHEST BIDDER

Government for Sale

Norman E. Wymbs

VANTAGE PRESS
New York

FIRST EDITION

Published by Vantage Press, Inc.
516 West 34th Street, New York, New York 10001

Manufactured in the United States of America
ISBN: 0-533-09335-X

Library of Congress Catalog Card No.:90-90376

0 9 8 7 6 5 4 3 2 1

To the politician who just says "No"

Contents

Foreword

Although there has been remarkably little public outrage expressed at the deteriorating standards at all levels of government, public opinion polls do show a seriously declining respect for those in position to run our lives. Politicians who, in this modern world of electronics and rapid communication, have learned that they live and die by the public opinion polls are showing high anxiety over their images. Even though they continue to put on their plastic smiles and hearty personalities in public, behind the scenes they are desperately fighting to recoup. When you take note of the large amounts of money being spent on public relations campaigns attempting to gloss over their sleazy image, you know the situation is getting dicey!

Unfortunately, the political concern has not gotten so great that our leaders are ready to institute any meaningful reforms in the way they conduct their profession. Political spokesman, particularly in the abnormal atmosphere of Washington, are quite vocal in their condemnation of those outside Government who would attempt to subvert our great American system. In the philosophy of "The best defense is a strong offense," we are bombarded in excruciating detail with revelations of the scurrilous activities of thieving Savings and Loan operators, or devious brokerage firms who have undermined the very foundations of our great country. In these continuing and seemingly endless assaults on our visual and auditory sensibilities, the power elite, in able partnership with the public news media, would have us believe that all corruption and wrongdoing comes from without, while those within are valiantly fighting a losing battle for honor and decency.

The campaign scenario is calculated to have us writhing with indignation over the revelations concerning the Savings and Loan horrors of Charlie Keating, or the duplicity of the Drexel Burnham brokerage gang. We are exhorted to ready the rope and tree branch for the undistinguished appointed officials presiding over the HUD (U.S. Department of Housing and Urban Development) scandals and the diversion of millions of dollars in taxpayers' money in that caper. Again, the firing squad would not be unwarranted in retaliation for the ridiculous expenditure of public dollars for $200 hammers and thousand-dollar toilet seats.

Once we have our righteous anger to the boiling point, and are ready to seek vengeance against these well-publicized transgressions, our governmental leaders happily join our chorus and demand retribution. But, what about their participation in these sordid events? Aren't all these things taking place under their "watch"? Weren't we all taught, a long time ago, that the buck stops at the boss's desk? Aren't they the bosses?

Now we hear the plaintive wails coming from our distinguished elected representatives allowing as how we should not be holding them to an overly high set of moral standards and quality of performance just because they are public figures! It seems that what they are trying to tell us is that they should be entitled to a little bit of cheating, stealing, and lying without reprisal; after all, everybody else is doing it! If you buy that position, and are willing to assume that everybody lies, cheats, and steals with impunity, I suggest you close the book here and pass it along to someone else who sets a higher standard!

The position taken by many politicians is much the same as that reputed to the late, great political boss, Mayor Richard Daley of Chicago. The story, probably apocryphal, but often told, has the crusty old mayor warning subordinates, "I know you're going to be making out, but the first one who draws too much attention to his wealth will be out on his posterior!" (Terminology was cleaned up for our older readers.) Despite this wise admonition, it would appear that too much attention has already been drawn to the personal wealth and free-spending lives of the country's politically powerful, contributing to the distrust being expressed by the electorate.

By definition, there can be no act of bribery unless there is a briber and a bribee. There can be no influence peddling unless there is a possessor of influence and a buyer seeking it. A degree in business from Harvard is not necessary to understand there is no sale without both a buyer and a seller!

If Charlie Keating is guilty of buying government favors from Washington, someone has to be guilty of selling them. The apologists within our political system cannot claim a corrupt purchase and ignore the equally corrupt sale! All the smooth interviews on the Sunday morning TV shows or the slick public relations campaigns cannot erase the fact that Senators Cranston, Glenn, DeConcini, McCain and Riegle used their political and official power in Keating's behalf and coincidentally received substantial monetary favors from that gentleman and his associates. On a less public level there is a similar cause and effect when second-rate political insiders, such as Republican National Committee wheeler-dealer, William Taylor, grow wealthy through their inside influence and ability to bring political buyers and sellers together.

Can we really accept the sincerity of pious government leaders who shed copious public tears and wring their hands in anguish over the heavy cost of bailing out the corrupt Savings and Loan industry? Can we believe their deep sympathy for the thousands of small investors broken by the continuing scandal of the "junk bond" scams? We can, if we blind ourselves to the root causes behind these tragedies. We can throw our arms around our very own senators and congressmen in sympathy if we conveniently forget who created the regulatory laxity that brought on these scandals! Realistically, how can Congress shed its collective guilt in these areas? The frightening thing about it is that other equally scandalous problems loom on the horizon.

Continuing to protest their own personal high level of integrity is not enough to explain their collective failures. The same Congress that continues to assure us they will save us from the S & L robber barons were quick to let (former House Speaker) Congressman Jim Wright gently slip off the hook by resigning in the face of potentially major scandals linked to the S & L mess. This same clubby group gave (House Majority Whip) Congressman Tony Coelho a friendly sendoff as he resigned in the face of a really smelly "junk bond" connection. Quick now, can you recall hearing any indignant rhetoric from the "oh so pure" members of Congress about the way those two slipped away? We shouldn't allow the heady aroma of manure surrounding our Congress to hide the fact that there are equally odoriferous examples of political buying and selling taking place outside those hallowed halls. The sad fact is that precious little takes place within our political system, in or out of government, that doesn't involve a substantial exchange of cash between those with the power and those purchasing it.

As we move along, we'll concern ourselves with the reasons behind our present state of government. Can our system continue to work as well as it has over the past two centuries without some major tinkering? How did we get to our current state? Was it something the Founding Fathers could have foreseen?

As it always is with any human endeavor, the system by itself cannot be the whole problem; we must consider the human equation. To do that we must take a close look at the backgrounds and personalities of the principal players. Would the "Keating Five" have performed as they did if there had been no Charlie Keating? Could Keating have gone as far as he did without those collaborating senators? Could a mediocre political party official gain wealth and power if the system were not set up for it? Would our executive division of government lead us differently if key players could not buy their positions? To put it all in perspective, suppose we *all* had the ability to get the ear of our senators to the extent that Charlie Keating did.

Whatever your personal feeling about your very own congressman or senators and the level of their performance on your behalf, I don't think you can escape the fact that something has gone wrong within the system. There used to be a running joke in vaudeville where the comedian intoned that "We have the best government that money can buy!" Unfortunately, that no longer is a joke.

Do we really want a government that is "Sold to the Highest Bidder"?

SOLD TO THE HIGHEST BIDDER

Chapter 1

Introduction

A truism, although used so frequently that it sounds trite, is that we cannot understand the present without a thorough knowledge of the past. This is especially true as we examine and puzzle over the present state of politics and government in the United States. Although we will be concentrating on the deplorable state of affairs in Washington and our national leadership, we cannot ignore the fact that every problem at the top level nationally is reflected proportionately throughout every level from statehouses to local courthouses.

The keystone of our present system of government is our two-party political adversary process. Although the founding fathers, at the birth of our nation, never discussed it or even gave any indication they understood the concept, their every move laid the foundations for our present Republican and Democrat parties. As a matter of fact, many historians, in retrospect, admit that the constitutional system hammered out in those sweaty days in old Philadelphia could not have functioned if the party system had not developed almost immediately thereafter.

Over the years our political parties have burgeoned well beyond the limits and functions originally incorporated in their formation. The early political antagonists would be hard put to recognize the highly secretive, tightly organized, and extremely wealthy organizations that the political parties have grown into today.

The competitive nature of our electoral system, a natural outgrowth of the drive and ambition behind the early development of this colony of Great Britain, was as normal to the writers of the Constitution as the lacing up of boxing gloves was to Jack Dempsey. The gentlemanly—and frequently scholarly—approach to government did not survive much beyond the Constitutional Convention of those first years. Given the nature of fierce competition over economic and personal issues early on, it was natural that alliances would develop to accomplish mutual goals. Frequently those alliances divided families, neighbors, and even church congregations, vitally important in the early history of the country.

We cannot, in today's materialistic society, begin to understand the highly charged battles over principles, such as the slavery-antislavery debates. Current confrontations over the human abortion issue raise passions to a degree, but most debates are muted by the underlying realization that our own individual economic concerns take precedence. In our country's formative years political issues took on the importance of pure religious dogma, with participants ready to fight and die for their positions. Today, principles are not anywhere near the most important issue. That is best illustrated, again, by the abortion issue, as the Democrat Party, which embraces abortion rights, and the Republican Party, which embraces the pro-life position, each scramble publicly to let us all know they accept both viewpoints in their membership.

There is good reason for this change in the underlying passion of commitment within our political party structure. To view it truly in perspective we must look at past history and compare it to our system today. From that comparison we have to face the ultimate question: Can a little adjusting correct our flaws, or are we facing major surgery?

Chapter 2
Foundation

Although we tend to accept it as a quasi-religious dictum that our country has a government "by the people and for the people," our understanding of the intent of our forefathers in those ringing words doesn't really match with what they had in mind for their new country. We prefer to think that we have a governing system freely and openly run by the collective will of all the people. We pretend that our divergent economic, intellectual, racial, and religious backgrounds blend together into a harmonious whole to run the country for the equal benefit of all. While these are truly beautiful thoughts, lending themselves well to impassioned speeches on patriotic holidays, they are at variance with the facts as they were conceived at the founding of our country. The very loose amalgamation of sovereign colonies hanging together after the War of Independence were led by strong-willed men who had very fixed concepts as to how a united country should function. These historic figures were not shy about expressing their opinions concerning who they thought should exercise the power in government. In that respect, it is difficult to see any differences in the feelings of those who now run the country both publicly and behind the scenes.

You need not be a historian, or a learned professor of government, to recognize that the engineers of our revolt and of ultimate independence from England were far from ordinary men. A cursory reading of the masterful United States Constitution they structured will leave even the most jaundiced in awe of their intellect. But then, this vast country, so diverse in geography and climate, could itself hardly be considered ordinary. In past history, countries naturally formed from groups of people with common backgrounds who lived in close proximity, but the United States was the first to arise from more unlikely roots. With hardly enough people to make up a decent-sized city, but covering a geographic area so vast that early Europeans thought it literally had no boundaries, it was presumptuous to assume this group of frontier colonies could ever become a viable, functioning nation.

The new confederation of states, in 1781, barely contained a combined total of 3 million inhabitants! In those fiercely independent territories, numbering thirteen and existing only through sheer chance of exploration, over 600,000 of those 3 million souls were indentured black slaves purchased from African dealers. The largest metropolitan area was Philadelphia, with 30,000 inhabitants, with New York trailing well behind in second place. Over 90 percent of the population, including virtually all the slaves, lived on farms.

Of the less than 2.5 million full-fledged citizens (black slaves didn't count), there was a wide gap between the wealthy, highly educated citizen and what we like to call today the "common man." In a striking difference from today, there was no middle class, just rich and poor. Although the New World had been settled largely by those who disagreed with England, their opposition to the old system was less political than it was economic. The great spread between the power of the wealthy and those less well-off in the mother country kindled a burning desire on the part of the "outs" to acquire wealth and power of their own. Because of the long-entrenched economic and social system in the Old World, there was little opportunity for ambitious have-nots to rise to the top of the system. The New World, to those long denied the benefits of the inner circle, looked like a happy hunting ground. Just the tempting prospect of becoming a big fish in the new pond was enough to draw talented potential leaders away from the rigid feudal system in their home countries. It didn't take long for the natural abilities and drive of those early entrepreneurs to become evident as they prospered and acquired wealth in the new land. They did so well, as a matter of fact, that in America the spread between the wealthy and the poor became even greater than in the Old Country.

In our present urban-oriented society, it's hard to picture the rural start of the United States. Most of the population was in farming, or other land-related enterprises, and most of the wealth being accumulated came from that area. That is not to say our early leaders were the humble hoe wielders and plow followers often shown in the old history books. Remember that those black slaves, representing more than 20 percent of the population, were mostly on the farms. Rapidly rising leaders, such as George Washington and Thomas Jefferson, were large farmers of their day. It would be ludicrous, however, to picture those learned gentlemen in the hot sun picking cotton or sweating behind a laboring horse. Washington, as a matter of fact, had over a hundred slaves assigned to household duties, besides the hundreds who did work in the fields! Without belaboring the point or trying to draw any moral line, it is important that we keep some of these facts in mind as we see how our political system evolved, and why it took the direction it did.

The fifty-five delegates to the Philadelphia Constitutional Convention were an excellent cross-section of the emerging leadership in the thirteen original colonies. None of these truly outstanding leaders and intellects could, in any way, be considered "ordinary," either by ability or economically. Fourteen of the assemblage were termed "land speculators." Here we're referring to men who, in those days, dealt in square miles, not acres! At least fifteen of the delegates were very large land owners and, of course, substantial slave owners. It took substantial holdings and wealth to buy and support private slave labor forces numbering into the hundreds of individual workers. Also, of passing interest, proving nothing much has changed over the years, thirty-four of the delegates were lawyers. Even then, the practice of law was the preferred profession from which to grow wealthy and politically powerful. All in all, here was a group of men who were outstandingly successful in their personal lives, very well-off economically, who mostly shared similar views and personal values. Financial independence, as a matter of practicality, was a prerequisite, since they had to pay their own way to, and stay in, Philadelphia—already a very expensive city.

Those fifty-five toiling, arguing, and sweating delegates were not politically powerful because they were there to write a Constitution; their power arose from their home territories. From a scattered and disorganized group of independent states they derived their clout from the fact they were, without elections or appointments, already the leaders in fact of their constituencies. A reading of the original Declaration of Independence, crafted by much of this group, clearly illustrates their mastery of the English language. Even more outstanding was their uncanny ability to communicate complex ideas in an easily understood text. Try comparing their clear, brief, and understandable language to the kind of gobbledygook pouring from thousands of governmental agencies today!

Looking back on the progress of the nation up to that point, and knowing the contentious backgrounds of the colonies, it is mind-boggling to note what they produced. From the very start it appeared impossible that they would come up with a system that even remotely approached the grandiose promise of "by the people," and "for the people," not to mention "of the people"!

The simple truth behind the deliberations and planning to establish a new government was that the architects never intended that government should be totally "of the people." In their very firm thinking, contrary to our romanticized version, the writers of the Constitution generally agreed that they, or others of similar cultural or educational background, were the only ones qualified to lead. It was all right to generalize that government should be of the people, but let's be sure that's only the "right" people! The "common" man could have the vote, but ruling was something else again. This elitist attitude was such a natural part of their thinking and culture that the subject didn't even require any form of open discussion during the planning.

The Continental Congress, theoretically acting as a representative ruling body of the thirteen colonies, but in reality about as effective and powerful as the present-day United Nations, had been meeting in New York City since the end of the Revolutionary War. Despite all their time in raucous argument and posturing, much like today's international body, they had been totally unable to come up with any semblance of unity. But, again, much like today's United Nations, their ineffective grandstanding was doted over by a delighted press who, with full access to their meetings, wrote yards and yards of copy, and quoted the participants endlessly. The only positive accomplishment of that Continental Congress was that they underscored the absolute need and urgency of the Constitutional Convention and their charge to develop the blueprint for a working government.

The organizers of the convention in Philadelphia took full note of the adverse effect of the media publicity in New York at the Congress, and elected to hold their meetings in full secrecy. Let it be noted that the media raged long and loud over this exclusion, but who, today, would deny that much of the probable political posturing was also excluded by this policy.

The cooler heads within the leadership of the independent states realized they must come up with a plan for a strong central government if the union were to survive. The states were already at each other's throats, maneuvering constantly for economic and territorial advantage. Armed clashes across the borders of some states were not uncommon.

The super-delegates in Philadelphia labored under no misapprehensions about the importance and urgency of their mission;

it was a matter of life and death for the union. They had to draw the participants into a unity of purpose and common cause, without giving up precious independence. The task was made all the more urgent by the specter of England, poised at the Canadian border, ready and itching for the first opportunity to move back and reclaim their colonies. Adding to the nail-biting situation was an aggressive Spain, with de facto control of everything west of the Mississippi, casting lustful looks toward the East. To put it mildly, the delegates' constituents back home were on edge and applying considerable pressure on their spokesmen to get cracking in Philadelphia.

The meetings in Philadelphia were conducted under such incredibly difficult conditions that it is a wonder anything at all was accomplished. The delegates, justifiably proud of their prestigious positions, conducted all their sessions in strict formality. Their formal attire, even fussier that today's congressional uniform of dark suit, white shirt, and conservative necktie, was hardly suited to the stifling heat of that summer in the Pennsylvania city. The tough climatic conditions, along with their almost paranoid desire for secrecy, was made even more intolerable as they held all meetings behind tightly closed doors and shuttered windows. Can you picture our present-day prima donnas in Washington showing the same fortitude and productive ability, were they forced to meet in closed rooms with no air conditioning? Hardly. Our guys and gals don't even meet during the heat of summer, despite their well-cooled quarters!

All of this enforced pomp in their deliberations reflected their unswerving belief that they were the "royalty" of the colonies and must, at all costs, maintain the courtly demeanor standard to the royal courts of Europe. This overriding concern for proper appearances was typically English elitism. They were all steeped in the Old Country's tradition whose leaders dressed formally for dinner even in jungle tents. Within the closed-door meetings, the "federalists" (favoring a strong central government) were in running conflict with the "statists," sometimes referred to as "republicans" (willing to yield only a minimum of their state's powers to a new central government). Despite strong ideologic clashes in this area, there was a universally urgent sense of the need to reach a compromise on a truly unified central government. Meanwhile, back in New York, the Continental Congress continued its ineffectual squabbling. The vaudeville show in that other city did perform an important function, however, in drawing away public attention from the Continental Congress where the real thinkers were free to deliberate in their sealed oven.

Into what had begun to look like a hopeless deadlock between the federalists and republicans, the delegates from Virginia brought a suggested outline. The Virginians, acknowledged to be the dominant force at the meeting, with their own George Washington sitting as a non-debating chairman, presented what was to become known as the "Virginia Plan" in an attempt to get things moving. Surprisingly, the outline was accepted by the delegates as a foundation for discussion, and it held up, largely intact, through the length of the convention.

The Virginia Plan was quickly grasped and understood by a majority of the delegates. Far from being concerned about keeping their religion separate from their politics, the personal faith of these men weighed heavily in all their deliberations. Most of them were devout members, and leaders, of churches back home. Most of their religious institutions were Protestant, deeply conservative, and decidedly fundamental in philosophy. It came as no surprise, then, when the Virginia Plan proposed a federal government based heavily upon the organization of the Presbyterian Church.

Remember, this group of delegates were the social and intellectual elite of their communities, and since the Presbyterian was the most elite of all local churches, familiarity bred acceptance! The Presbyterian governing body consisted of the deacons (in some churches, called trustees) whose function was to raise funds for the church, run the day-to-day secular operations of the organization, and to supervise the staff to get the job done. The deacon positions were generally filled from the hardworking, devoted members of the congregation who had the skills to keep the organization running smoothly.

The elders of the presbytery were the true elite of the congregation (even today the generic term "elder" is applied to those who have exhibited a level of leadership and statesmanship above that of the ordinary man). This select and revered group decided high policy of the church and had the responsibility of choosing the minister (actually, "chief elder"). The minister held full responsibility for the executive management of the church and was the public spokesman for the congregation.

In the original Virginia Plan, the deacons became the House of Representatives, the elders became the Senate and the chief elder, the President. In the only major change from the original plan, after long debate, the delegates decided to remove the selection of the President from the Senate. The larger states feared the smaller states would have too much power with their equal votes in the Senate. The new plan designated the House of Representatives as the deciding body, through the unique system of the Electoral College.

It's easy to see, in retrospect, why this basic governmental system, lifted unashamedly from the Presbyterian Church, had such appeal to the Convention delegates. George Washington, along with many of his associates from Virginia and elsewhere, was a Presbyterian by upbringing. The church that his family belonged to when he grew up still stands in Fredericksburg, Virginia. The Washington family pew still has the brass nameplate testifying to their ownership of the seats. The pews were always sold to prominent members of the congregation, the family's status being indicated by the location of these permanently reserved seats. The Washington pew, not unexpectedly, is in the front of the church.

In the secluded, elite world from which these delegates came, the church served as a stabilizing social influence, much like the exclusive clubs of old England. Their social lives and personal friendships, from birth to death, revolved around their churches. Despite some very sharp differences in political philosophy and governmental preferences, their general unity in religious belief drew the delegates together like nothing seen since. There was little difference in governing organization and faith between the Protestant denominations most of them belonged to. More importantly, particularly with the dominant Presbyterian and Episcopal Churches, membership and organization provided an easy way to separate the truly elite from the ordinary folks. It was impossible for anyone outside the exclusive inner group to be chosen as an elder of his church. This was what they all wanted for their new country.

On that one issue all the delegates were very much in accord; they wanted to be sure the government of their country was run by "proper" people and not taken over by riffraff as happened in France after their revolution. Many of these men had grown up in England, or had been educated in proper English schools and were accustomed to a country run by royalty and staffed by a handpicked, elite group of administrators. Their lifelong indoctrination dictated that government should always be kept in the hands of those who were intellectually and socially suited to leadership. The fact that they had broken away from the mother country represented not so much a rejection of these basic tenets as it did a frustrated desire to be one of the ruling elite.

Generally they had no overwhelming desire to return to anything resembling a monarchy, although there was a substantial effort mounted to name George Washington king. It was only the inherent good sense of Washington that kept them from going that route. An honest desire to open up government, while at the same time not letting the reins of control out of the hands of those truly qualified to lead, brought about the final acceptance of the modified Virginia Plan. The majority of delegates felt comfortable with the Senate setup as providing the best method for the central government to be protected from those they saw as unqualified to govern. They were secure in the knowledge that in this new union only the highly educated, cultured, and wealthy individual could possibly reach the lofty goal of United States Senator.

As the new nation began to shape up under its carefully drawn Constitution, it appeared that the founding fathers' concerns about qualified people were unfounded. The government was forming up nicely with an elitist class at the helm. Although they were not established by Old World family lines, they still constituted a ruling group with very narrow qualifications. This emergence of a ruling class showed up quite clearly as the first rudimentary political parties began to appear. Although much, on the surface at least, has changed since those early years, the elitist thread has remained unbroken from Philadelphia to this day.

Chapter 3
Birth of the Parties

After the Constitution was satisfactorily in place, the new United States elected George Washington its first President, without opposition. The political euphoria over the fledgling government and its Revolutionary War hero president lasted until the first Congress convened. With the weighty problems concerning the nation's structural form settled, the even more difficult task of actual governing had to be faced. It didn't take long for the honeymoon that followed Washington's inauguration to come to an end.

George Washington, himself largely responsible for bringing the new states together, was unabashedly an advocate for a strong, if not domineering, central government. On the opposite political tack sailed his old friend and debating opponent, Thomas Jefferson. Jefferson was the leading and most eloquent spokesman for even more independence for the states. It didn't take long for the two viewpoints to divide Congress and the administration into opposing political and philosophical camps. Alexander Hamilton, Washington's Treasury Secretary, championed the federalists' cause, mainly through his advocacy of a strong central banking system. Jefferson, Washington's Secretary of State, carried the Republicans' banner holding out for the states to control monetary policy through their own banking systems. That philosophical battle naturally expanded in Congress with Jefferson's fellow Virginian and political ally, James Madison, eloquently handling the debate for the states' rightists.

These first ideological clashes quickly led to heated shouting matches on the floors of Congress, much to the distress of the participants themselves. The gentlemanly cultural backgrounds of these early leaders, and their normally courtly demeanor, required that they work out their differences behind closed doors so as to maintain formal and altogether proper public relationships in the halls of Congress. That overwhelming desire for decorum at any cost laid the foundation for the transparently phony gentlemanly conduct still on public display in today's legislative halls.

Jefferson, especially, deplored most open debate, to the extent that when he saw the debaters were crossing the line of propriety, he simply withdrew. He felt very strongly that real gentlemen resolved their differences in private. In this he represented the feelings of most of the legislators who were convinced that ordinary people could not possibly understand the complexity of the issues Congress confronted. Most of them agreed that no matter how vituperative the discussions became in private, a unified demeanor in public was essential. This historic attitude continues even today, only now we have learned to sugar-coat the terminology. The "button-down collar" image makers of today will not let our political leaders do anything so crass as "cutting a deal" behind the scenes: instead, they hammer out statesmanlike compromises. No matter the term, however, the deals are still being made and they're still in the back room behind closed doors!

The local campaigns where the candidates had to face the public were difficult to keep on the high plane the early leaders so coveted. By 1792 politics in the trenches was already getting rough, and although there were no outward signs of formal political party alignments taking place, the governing elitists were beginning to put organizations together.

Communication was the most critical problem in those first years. Getting the message to the voter was no easy task, considering the primitive state of the news media. By the time the irregular mails or scattered newspapers got the political message to the outlying precincts, most of the major elections were already over. This did not present as great a problem in most of the southern states, since they only had to worry about local elections for the state legislatures. Once the legislatures convened, they chose the state's governor and U.S. senators. The northern states, however, were set up for direct public election of their top positions by statewide popular votes. With broadly spread public voting, transmitting the political dogma to the far-flung, mostly unsophisticated voters was a real challenge. New York State was the first to attack this problem with the formation of "Committees of Correspondence," organized groups who relayed the instructions as to whom to support in the elections. The voters, for the most part, did not know the candidates or have any say in their selection. The political insiders who formed the "Committees" handpicked the candidates without competition and then spread the word for their support. Thus, the early, faceless political power brokers arrived on the scene.

With New York in the forefront of these first small steps toward formal political parties, the southern states with their already tightly controlled elections found no need to follow suit. Virginia—oddly enough New York's strongest ally in the republican movement—had the most tightly organized general elections in the country. "Committees," such as New York's, were unneeded since their local legislative candidates already came out of the socioeconomic elite of their society; improper candidates dared not run for office. These legislators, naturally, only chose proper persons for the positions of governor or senator.

In 1796, during the election of John Adams, real political parties finally began to emerge as forces to be reckoned with. As the Madison-Jefferson combine became more open in their opposition to the Washington-Adams forces, both sides had to develop more formalized and disciplined organizations. By this time they had learned to use the clout of their federal and local positions to force state and community leaders to declare their political allegiance before general elections were held. Word was firmly passed down the line as to who would be the favored choices of the two major factions. These power plays began to force local issues into the background as local candidates had to campaign "with" Adams or Jefferson. The local power brokers were informed they had better exercise all their economic and social clout behind the scenes for the favored candidates, or face possible retaliation from the powers at the rapidly strengthening federal level. Although Jefferson had, by far, the better organized political machine, the personal popularity of outgoing President Washington prevailed and his handpicked successor, John Adams, won the election. In recent history we witnessed the same strength of personal popularity as a lackluster George Bush won election because of public affection for outgoing president Ronald Reagan.

Thomas Jefferson, the consummate politician, was well aware of the reason for his defeat, and during the ensuing years as Adams's vice president, devoted himself to expanding and strengthening his political organization.

Blatantly using the power of his office as vice president under his archrival Adams, Jefferson concentrated on building his machine to ultimately topple the president. Although the office of vice president had no real power under the Constitution, Jefferson himself was so personally popular and of such national stature that he created clout in the job. Now the Jefferson followers, variously referred to as "Republicans" or "Democrat Republicans" openly aligned themselves against the "Federalist" supporters of President Adams.

By 1800, Jefferson's forces, mostly southern, had drawn into a tightly controlled and organized political party. In that year they printed and circulated what might be loosely termed the first official party platform. Establishing wh... has become a long-lived tradition, their platform offered nothing of any concrete substance. Those Republicans promoted themselves as the party of "things as they will be," all good of course, as opposed to the Federalists as the party of "things as they have been," naturally quite bad!

Adding to the many noteworthy accomplishments as a writer and one of the founders of the nation, Jefferson can also be credited with the now long time political standby, the half-truth! In a campaign White Paper put out by the Republicans opposing the Federalists of George Washington, he emphasized, "We will not raise your taxes!" while alongside, in bold print, "They (Federalists) raised your taxes!" Crassly ignored in this first recorded Political half-truth was the fact that no taxes at all existed prior to George Washington's administration, since there had been no government to impose them! As the new government imposed levies to pay for its operation, technically they "raised taxes," going from nothing to something!

In 1840, the Jefferson Democrat Republicans, meeting in the country's first formal political convention, officially named themselves the "Democrat Party." The Washington Federalists, vacillating between "National Republican" and "Whig" as their title, finally met in 1854 and formally took the title "Republican Party." Coincident with their meeting, they nominated Abraham Lincoln as their first presidential candidate. Besides finally having developed full-fledged political organizations with distinctive names, the Republicans and Democrats drew sharp lines between their philosophical differences.

The Republicans, true to the early standards of George Washington, held firmly to the concept of a strong central economic and monetary policy and a strong unified national military force. The Democrats, equally loyal to the aristocratic Jeffersonian tradition, strongly opposed federal intervention into what they considered purely state prerogatives. The formalizing and hardening of the philosophical differences between the political parties, as much as anything else, was to lead to the devastating Civil War.

The holocaust of the War between the States, besides destroying the institution of slavery once and for all, solidified the central government of the United States and started it on its way to becoming a world economic and political power. The country was no longer a loosely amalgamated collection of rural colonies but a unified industrial trendsetter. Some very important but largely unnoticed changes also took place within the political organizations of the Union.

Party leaders from the start and through the early 1800s were mostly the wealthy plantation owners and the intellectual gentry. This elite group ran their organizations quietly, albeit ruthlessly, behind the scenes. After the early years of Washington, Jefferson, and Adams, the political power brokers were content to maintain low profiles while their handpicked public officeholders basked in the spotlight. To their credit, in the beginning they sought not only qualifications but high character in their choices to run for public office. Unfortunately, the overriding demand for "electability" gradually supplanted all other considerations.

The advent of the industrial revolution after the Civil War brought a whole new breed into the insider political power structure. Replacing the older intellectuals and "blue bloods," newly rich and powerful businessmen and developers elbowed in and took control of the political machines. On the surface, at least to the rank and file, everything seemed the same. The insiders still screened and selected the candidates for office and then put the party volunteer organizations to work promoting their election. The key factor now, however, was money. No longer were qualifications and integrity the primary criteria in choosing candidates. The candidate who could show the strongest financial backing, and ultimately guarantee the maximum financial return on the investment, got the nod from the party insiders. Now the power brokers were looking for something more than good government from their choices.

During the years between the Civil War and World War I, the powerful men behind the scenes made one of their most important moves towards control of public opinion and the ultimate election of their chosen candidates. Many of these insiders, already wealthy from their endeavors, turned towards newspapers as a sideline occupation and means to consolidate their power base. Newspapers, with telegraph systems to speed major news stories rapidly, and widespread rail transportation to spread their publications, were springing up across the whole country. No longer were a few major metropolitan papers able to control the printed word. These papers were more oriented toward news and strong editorial opinions than the bundles of advertising print we are accustomed to. The new publishers made no bones about their political positions, and within their own controlled pages allowed no dissent from their party line. There was no pretense of being fair by presenting the other side; as you read them you saw there was no other side! To make sure the reader fully understood where they were coming from they usually included the terms "Republican" or "Democrat" in the titles on their mastheads. Many of these titles continue today, although without the unabashed political affiliation of the earlier years. What a shocker it would be if today's newspapers, or TV networks were as honest in revealing their agendas.

With the 1800s coming to a close, the two major political parties were firmly established as traditional American institutions. Individuals had learned to identify with the label of their political party with all the fervor of a religious faith. Much like their religion, most of the voters claiming political party affiliation did so by reason of birth or social background rather than because of any strong philosophical conviction. That strong, unthinking loyalty had a profound effect on the entire electoral process in the United States.

Straight party voting was the norm; the candidate at the top of the ticket invariably carried all of his party into office at most levels. Astoundingly, with such little individual thought being given to the individual candidates by the voters, the turnout at the polls consistently topped 80 to 90 percent! This was a period of euphoria for political party insiders. Once they decreed who the candidates would be, they could rest comfortably knowing no outsider would dare challenge their designated office holders, and the electorate would dutifully vote the party line.

Paradoxically, the political parties, while at the peak of their electoral power, had also acquired their worst public images. Cartoonists made whole careers out of depicting potbellied political bosses, puffing on the inevitable black cigar, meeting secretly to anoint the future officeholders and leaders of the country. This image became so strong that a permanent image in our culture of the "smoke-filled room" has become symbolic of the shady secret deal.

This phase of our national politics continued into the early part of this century when the old system had to face a new challenge. The advent of more, and better, newspapers, followed by the explosive growth of radio put the insiders' political system to its greatest test. With worldwide events now common household topics, and two major world wars, public heroes were being created almost faster than the country could absorb them. It was predictable that these nationally known figures would gravitate toward politics and public office as a means of remaining in the limelight. Now the background political powers were faced with individuals from outside their closed system who could challenge for public office on their own. Many of these individuals showed such powerful public appeal that they transcended any organizational power within the Republican or Democrat parties. If these personalities were to make it on their own, what was to happen with the clout of the old manipulators?

The most notable of this new breed of national candidate was General Dwight Eisenhower, a genuine national hero and household name arising from the Allied victory in World War II. He needed no campaign strategy or political organization; all he needed to get elected was to show up! For the first time the two major political parties had met their match, they both openly courted Ike to be their candidate. Public personality was acknowledged to be more important than political philosophy.

When Ike won the presidency totally on his own merits and reputation, he entered office owing nothing to the Republican Party that had won his endorsement. President Eisenhower's eight years in office did more to shake up our political system than anything since the advent of Abe Lincoln!

To survive, the political parties had to shift gears and tactics after Ike. Ironically, while the growth of radio had been a major contributor to the cracking of the old insider system, the new electronic medium of television was to provide the means for the backroom powers to make a comeback. With that revival has come a level of blatant corruption and vote-buying far beyond the wildest dreams of the old cigar chomping "smoke-filled room" wheeler-dealers!

Chapter 4
The Political Machines

The national political parties have developed over the years into a pyramidal structure closely resembling the governments with which they have a close symbolic relationship. The broad base of the pyramid consists of the widespread precinct and county committees where most of the dedicated and idealistic volunteers toil for their concept of good government.

This broad base rapidly grows away from pure idealism toward hard-nosed political pragmatism as the pyramid narrows up toward the state committee organizations. By the time you reach the middle management level of politics, the dedicated volunteers are rapidly replaced by ambitious young professionals and self-serving power brokers. At the point of the overall structure, in Washington, where both national party committees are based, you encounter the real meat in the system.

Although the honest labor and organizational work emanates from the base of the pyramid at the precinct and county levels, all the party policies and most of the personal rewards derive from the peak in Washington. That this is no amateur or part-time game is best illustrated by the level of security surrounding the top-secret operations of both the Republican and Democrat national headquarters. It is only slightly less difficult penetrating beyond the reception desks at these bases of political power than it would be to pay a casual visit to Fort Knox or even the CIA Headquarters in suburban Washington. Even telephone contacts are carefully screened and employees strictly censored in what they can say to outsiders. We'll look at those phenomena a little later.

The big question is, how do the top-level managers of the system get to the point where they hold that pyramidal power, and why are they so secretive about it? Before looking at what they are hiding, let's look at how they got there.

At the local, base level, most political party committees are chosen through precinct elections or caucuses. These, with few exceptions, are the true volunteers in political party activism. These committee members, along with local political club members, devote untold spare hours of their time towards the repetitive and labor-intensive tasks connected with local election campaigns. Usually, at this level, there is a strong personal link between the candidates for public office and their volunteer election workers. Unfortunately for the whole system, this close personal tie between the future officeholder and working volunteers exists only at the lowest electoral level. As campaigns broaden out for the higher elective offices, the personal contact disappears. Along with it disappears the high level of enthusiasm and dedication found in the lower campaign efforts. But what about those few exceptions at the lower party level who don't approach political activity as a volunteer project on behalf of idealistic principles only?

There are those who recognize the opportunities beckoning from the higher party levels but who, out of necessity, must start at the bottom to get there. Later on we'll take a look at the privileged group, a majority in both parties, who start at the very top and how they manage that feat. At the entry level you can easily spot those who seek more than the opportunity to put in long volunteer hours for a political cause. They are the ones who actively, often ruthlessly, campaign for the beginning positions. It is not out of the ordinary for these ambitious few to conduct professional and quite expensive campaigns for those positions where less than a thousand voters participate in the elections or caucuses.

There is nothing in the way of real personal reward available to those participants at the entry level, but those positions do put the holders in the forefront to move up into the big-time of inside politics. Continuing up the ladder, the ambitious political neophyte's next move is to his party's state central committee. Here are encountered the first indications of the lucrative possibilities for political service on the inside. Most state committees are composed of from 150 to several hundred members representing counties or political subdivisions.

It is not unusual for individuals seeking these state committee seats to spend $50,000 or more on their campaigns! As an indication of how well these inside party positions and their function are isolated from any public scrutiny, there are no laws or party rules requiring disclosure of money spent on these campaigns. When someone is willing to put up thousands of dollars to get people into, what appear on the outside at least, to be insignificant party positions you do have to become curious as to what they expect from the investment.

At the state committee level in the political game, many of the party officials draw handsome salaries and expense allowances from funds donated to the party. Any state party chairman, for example who does not draw at least $50,000 plus perks annually is being snookered by the insiders. Free automobiles and ample travel accounts are the norm in many state party positions below the level of chairman as well. Annual operating budgets in excess of $10 million, all supposedly from volunteer donations to the party, are not uncommon at the state level.

The members of these state committees choose from among themselves a state chairman and two additional members to serve on the party's national committee in Washington. The competition for these positions is hot and heavy, and no holds are barred in maneuvering for these personally rewarding slots. In California, campaigning for state chairman of the Democrat Party reached new heights. Former California Governor Jerry (Moonbeam) Brown, out of the public eye for a number of years, waged a powerful campaign for that position as head of only one of the more than fifty state and territorial Democrat committees. Party spokesmen in California reported that Brown spent in excess of $300,000 in his successful quest to be chairman of their party. Considering that this sum was expended only to garner the less than 1,000 votes from the committee to secure the position, had George Bush spent proportionally the same amount per vote earned, his successful presidential campaign would have cost in excess of $15 billion.

Moving into the heady reaches of the national political committees, access to any real information about what goes on behind their sealed doors is well-nigh impossible. Occasionally someone leaks little tidbits, giving some indication of the lucrative positions available on the staffs of these committees. Political campaign veteran Ed Rollins was reported to have accepted a position in 1989 as co-chairman of the Republican Congressional Campaign Committee at a salary of $250,000 per year! It makes for intriguing speculation as to what others are getting paid when the co-chairman of a subcommittee of the Republican Party does that well.

Although the large salaries paid to the full-time inside employees of the parties makes for titillating discussion, that is not where the real financial benefits accrue. A better understanding of the opportunities available to the party insiders at the top level is gathered from reports leaked after the 1986 Republican senatorial campaign.

In that disastrous year for the Republican Party, a net of eight critical U.S. Senate seats were lost and control of that body went over to the Democrats. After that humiliating loss (with a Republican president in office, no less), the GOP Senatorial Campaign Committee (another subcommittee of the national party) declared over $225,000 in special bonuses to the leaders of the losing effort! While graciously accepting a $50,000 bonus for his less-than-sparkling leadership, Committee Executive Director Thomas Griscom also awarded a $90,000 bonus to the fund-raising firm he had employed during the campaign. This in itself was an outstanding gesture of generosity, considering the fund raisers, while already taking a handsome cut of the funds raised for themselves, did not raise enough money to cover the campaign's costs. In one of those coincidences that keep turning up in the inside world of politics, this "outside," highly paid, fund-raising firm happened to be owned by another paid employee of the GOP Committee, Executive Finance Director Rodney Smith!

Maybe you don't find this sort of self-dealing very shocking; obviously the Republican party leadership didn't, since these individuals weren't even reprimanded! The reason nothing was done is that this practice is commonplace within the inner sanctums of the parties. In my own home state, in recent years, the "outside" computer and direct-mail firms were owned by the very party officials and paid employees who retained them for the party. This kind of double-dipping by already paid employees of the political parties is unchallenged simply because the party insiders in command have even better deals going for themselves.

In Florida, recently, Jeannie Austin (now co-chairman to Lee Atwater of the Republican National Committee), upon retiring as Chairman of the Florida State GOP, received a $20,000 automobile as a going away gift. Some years earlier, the outgoing chairman of a local county committee not only received a new car but was also presented with a bank account containing $10,000! Pretty nice rewards for positions only held for a few years. Mrs. Austin will pop up later in our continuing narrative.

But, so what? Who cares if the insiders in our political system are so successful at lining their own pockets? It's no skin off your nose, is it? Before moving on, I suggest you gently rub your nose. Your pockets are being picked while you sit there smiling.

Chapter 5

Private Clubs?

Over the years there have been numerous attempts to force reform and open dealing upon the two major political parties. Although compelling arguments have been presented to state and federal courts showing that the two parties are instrumental in controlling who gets into public office, to the detriment of the electorate, the system remains unchanged. The Courts consistently maintain, in agreement with attorneys for both the Democrats and Republicans, that the political parties are no more than social clubs. Along that line they advise reformers, if you don't like it, quit and join another club!

If you will pause for a moment and try to view the Republican and Democrat National Committees as clubs, on the level of your local golf or bridge clubs, you may wonder where these judges are coming from. That may be answered when you also consider that all the judges arise from within the political system, and all of them, all the way to the Supreme Court, depend upon the political insiders for appointment to their positions.

Let's examine the powers of the political insiders in the parties and then compare that to the president of your own Kiwanis or Elks club! If the Demos and the GOP are indeed private social clubs, most of them exist in another society.

There are two major factors that take political parties out of the social category and show them for what they are—de facto, if not actual, governments within government.

If you read your junk mail regularly, you are well aware that both the Democrats and Republicans spend a great deal of time begging money for their committees. We are exhorted to mail our checks so that they may support worthy candidates of the party in their quest for public office. We are led to believe that our ten- or twenty-dollar bill will be applied directly to the election campaigns of those eminently qualified individuals. We've already seen that much of that freely donated money is stopped before it ever gets near a candidate for public office. You can rest easy, however, in the knowledge that your funds, at least, are helping the economy and providing a good life for someone!

Not as well publicized, however, is how they raise the great bulk of the many millions of dollars they have to promote their agendas. Contributions from individual contributors are important to the political organizations only in that they keep a large number of voters personally interested in their chosen party. The big money comes from individuals and groups who give thousands of dollars at a crack, and who do so anonymously. Contrary to the generally held belief that all political donations are reported to some official government agency, the preponderance of party funds are received and expended in secret. It is the control of the sources of these funds and how they are spent that confers the real power upon the Democrat and Republican insiders. We'll go into more detail later, but for now, keep in mind that we are talking about hundreds of millions of dollars! Unless you play a pretty heady game, this still doesn't sound much like your local bridge club, does it?

The other critical factor in the real power of the political parties is their control over who ultimately runs for public office. Although technically any citizen who is qualified can run for public office, in practice government office is only an idle dream for the unanointed. One of the most critically controlled functions of the political organizations from bottom to top is that of selecting acceptable candidates for office and excluding those that do not pass muster with the insiders. This screening process extends to the lowest elective level, even to those offices that by local law are officially nonpartisan. Party leaders are always on the lookout for suitable individuals who have the potential to eventually move into the most powerful state and federal offices.

In sifting through potential candidates, the most important criterion is controllability. The power brokers cannot afford to have officeholders who do not listen to their private counsel, and do not do as they are told. Next in importance is electability: there's no point in getting behind someone who can't be packaged and sold to an American public accustomed to quickly presented, attractive products.

But as important as it is to find candidates who will not rock the boat while at the same time are attractive enough to be elected, money is so paramount as to make the other factors only incidental. At the lowest political level, when party officials have their first secret meetings with potential candidates, the ambitious budding politician hardly has time to get his hat off before he's hit with the "money thing."

Question number one addressed to any candidate, from the lowest local race to the highest state or federal challenge, is, "How much money will you have for the campaign?" Most neophyte candidates are startled by this for many of them naively think that campaign money will come from their chosen political party. The initial indoctrination, especially for the first-timers, is to bluntly let them know they are not going to be able to campaign on party money. They quickly learn that the relatively small portion of general campaign funds coming from their political party is reserved for the established officeholders and the top state and federal positions. At the lower and starting levels the candidate must tap his own resources for funds.

Once accepted by the party insiders, the candidates are put through a series of high-intensity training sessions. Although, on the outside, the parties pretend these are to teach campaigning technique and organization, the number one priority, money, is never off the agenda. The candidate learns very quickly that his hopes and aspirations for public service are for nought unless he comes up with big money to finance the effort. He is exhorted to apply pressure to all his family and friends to kick into the campaign. The new candidate who shows strong connections to a major business association or union, capable of providing big bucks for his campaign is met with open arms by his party leaders. The training sessions make clear that he has little hope of progressing in the system if he expects to lean on his dedicated volunteer supporters to get him elected. He is quickly taught the importance of professional campaign handlers and particularly the need for high-powered media managers. It's a pretty dull potential officeholder who doesn't get the message early, "Forget everything else, raise the money!"

Put yourself in the shoes of one of these young, and probably new to politics, potential candidates. You've been active in your local civic club, or association. You've studied local issues and have become a spokesman for a special issue or philosophy. People are impressed by your eloquence and knowledge of things governmental, and many of them are urging you to run for office. Being new at the game, and caught up in the heady excitement of all that praise and encouragement, the voices of those early friends and supporters are multiplied a thousandfold in your mind, and the desire to run for office is born. At this stage you are thoroughly caught up in the righteousness of your mission, and know that everyone will flock to your crusade as soon as you make your positions known. Now you're ready to approach the leadership of the political party of your choice and announce your availability for public service!

Now you can understand the shock to most individuals who follow this common line into the political system and encounter the cold facts for the first time. Forget about issues, you learn early in the indoctrination, keep your public options open. Your primary function in the political loop is to generate large sums of money; the professionals will take care of getting you elected. You quickly learn that the inflow of money relates directly to what you promise to do for those supplying the funds. Suddenly you are faced with the realization that those friendly developers shaking your hand and offering checks at the private cocktail party are not signing on the dotted line with the expectation that you are going to be supporting what they consider to be an unfavorable land-planning act.

At this stage of the game, the political hopeful is faced with a major and irrevocable decision. If he sticks with his good instincts and stands firm on all his principles, he's outside the system and on his own in his political campaign. If he rationalizes, which is eminently easy to do, that those inside the party and the other special interest groups are really devoted to the public good, he will subvert his own positions and "go with the flow." Having decided with the system, he sets his future in concrete: from now on, most of his effort as a candidate, and later as an officeholder, will be devoted to "raise the money!"

Now the political party insiders are ready to embrace the candidate without reservation. Although they will not provide much money from their own big secret pot, they will direct the future officeholder into the right channels to tap the great rivers of free-flowing cash available from those seeking to have the inside track with government. Although the public does not know it, their favorite is now speaking more from the power of the dollars than from that of conviction.

This inside and tightly protected power to choose, indoctrinate, and provide financial sources for candidates for public office certainly removes the political parties from the category of "private club" that the courts insist they are. The more publicized methods devised to nominate candidates for major office are even further proof that political parties are truly governments within government. You need not look much beyond the overwhelming influence of such events as the farcical Iowa presidential nomination caucuses (set up by the party powers) to understand the electoral influence our Republican and Democrat private clubs have on our lives.

What about these public officeholders, however? Having learned early on that money is the root of all success, what are they to do? Obviously, all they can do is grub for the money, too frequently and at any cost, if they expect to be successful and remain in office. Our big concern, however, is not so much the cost of their political campaigns, as obscene as that is getting to be, but the effect it has on these individuals who day by day see so much free-flowing cash. Can we expect them to be pure enough to not succumb to the personal temptation posed by this system? Since many of them have already compromised their philosophical beliefs, can we expect them to hold to a high moral standard around all that money? It is almost impossible to be content with dry bread when all the insiders around you are enjoying cake and champagne!

The sale of the integrity of our governing process is like a rampaging virus that continually feeds on itself. As influence is bought, and riches made thereof, more buyers rush into the act. As more buyers surface, sales prices rise, and petty graft grows to be major corruption. As the epidemic spreads, the incidence of spectacular, newsworthy corruption increases. As the big headline cases, such as the rolling affair of the "Keating Five," arouse our indignation, just as many big buys are taking place without much public attention. We'll look at both categories.

Chapter 6
Who Is That Unmasked Man?

If this were a work of fiction and it became necessary to create a villain to illuminate the theme of corruption in government, no author could do better than the real-life character of Charlie Keating, Jr. Bursting upon the scene like a massive fireworks display, seemingly from nowhere, "Charlie" Keating and his failed Lincoln Savings, a California Savings and Loan company, have loomed larger than life for over a year in our national media.

Although there had been constant rumbles over recent years about the perilous condition of the nation's savings institutions, the news, as far as the public was concerned, had hardly reached the "ho-hum," "so what?" level. Our political leaders in Washington, ably abetted by the unmovable bureaucracy, who were actively participating in the swinging lifestyle of the S & L high rollers, kept the full extent of the approaching disaster under a tight lid of obfuscation. Even when the spoiled porridge boiled over and our reluctant leaders had to face the cleanup chore, the full details were withheld from the public. Amid assurances that depositors in the mortally ill industry would be protected from personal losses, our cowardly leaders distanced themselves from the raging infection by creating another bureaucracy to seek a cure. The "Resolution Trust Corporation" was brought into existence to try to clean up the mess the country's elected leadership did not want to face. Now we had a new government agency, rapidly bloating itself with personnel and offices, charged with undoing what Congress and the Executive branch had allowed to happen. This corrective action is estimated to represent an ultimate cost to the taxpayers of more than $500 billion! But still there was no serious outcry from the public concerning how all this came about! Just when it looked like the "good ol' boys" in Washington had dodged another bullet and could go back to fun and games as usual, up popped Charlie!

Charlie Keating's impact on the media, and subsequently on the public, is more a result of the bizarre personality and lifestyle of this tall, lanky character than it is his transgressions, although considerable, in the S & L industry. There are others who have exploited and benefitted personally from Congress's dereliction in oversight control of these major financial institutions to an extent equal to or greater than perpetrated by Charlie. For example, how much attention have you noted in the national media concerning a Mr. David Paul?

Mr. Paul ran the CenTrust Savings Bank in Florida as his personal fiefdom before federal regulators were forced to move in and shut him down. Although not as large as the estimated $3 billion required to bail out Keating's plaything, Paul's swinging operation is figured to cost the taxpayers over $1 billion! Mr. Paul, before being cut off at the pass, indulged in such tastes as private jet aircraft, chauffeured limousines, imported Persian rugs, priceless French art masterpieces, $120,000 dinner parties in his palatial home—and the ultimate in the good life—14-karat gold nails securing the decks of his private yacht! All of this comfortable living by Mr. Paul was with depositors' money (estimated at over $45 million) which now, of course, will be made up by Washington's taxpayer-funded Resolution Trust Corporation! Mr. Paul's sickening extravagance with other people's money is typical of many other industry exploiters all over the country that we hear little about. Still, with so little attention by the media and Congress to the "David Pauls" in the S & L racket, how did such a harsh spotlight get focused on Charlie Keating?

For one thing, you can safely bet the family mortgage money that there has been a generous sharing of the loot from the S & L collapse, between the robber barons and our political leaders. Most of those being caught with their hands in this till, once thought bottomless, have elected to ride quietly off into the sunset with their personal gains, leaving the shambles behind for the taxpayers to clean up. What has been different about the Keating caper is that he refused to mount up and ride away! Unwilling to let the insiders just hand him the gun, instructing him to "do the right thing" as they quietly closed the door, Charlie elected to challenge them all to meet him down at the old corral. Adding to the excitement of this impending duel is the fact that Charlie didn't just deal with your run-of-the-mill Washington influence peddlers, he worked his deals only with the top echelons of the power system. The U.S. senators, prominently linked with Charlie's free-swinging and fast-moving enterprises, constitute a veritable "Who's Who" of Washington.

Senator Alan Cranston of California, venerable Democrat leader who for years has been untouchable by Republican opponents, stands out as one of Charlie's boys. Senator John Glenn of Ohio, genuine American hero astronaut and a serious contender for his party's presidential nomination, and Senator Dennis DeConcini of Arizona, himself often touted as presidential timbre, were charter members of Charlie's Angels. Senator Donald Riegle, Jr., of Michigan, with a long and carefully cultivated image of statesmanship, and neophyte, but presidentially ambitious, Senator John McCain of Arizona, round out the Keating insider connection in Washington. This esteemed group, despite long years of effort trying to make a positive mark in history, seem doomed to be remembered through posterity only as members of the "Keating Five," the title so aptly coined by the media!

The "Keating Five," for crying out loud—who is this guy who so suddenly acquired the status of a household name? With what we've already discussed, and more to come later, we'll see why Charlie may well take a place in history even *he* never dreamed of! Sadly, our whole political system is so rife with corruption that were there no real Charlie Keating out there, the Keating Five and others like them would have been forced to invent one! A closer look at this larger-than-life character, and his ability to buy government for his own personal use, is warranted at this time.

Charles H. Keating, Jr., son of an ordinary middle-class couple in Cincinnati, Ohio, had nothing in his background to indicate his future status as a household name. The only thing that any of his peers from those early years can remember is that he had more than his share of drive and aggression. In retrospect, and knowing him today, you would agree he was, and is, a classic case of hyperactivity! With his acknowledged and now fully visible desire to be always in the forefront, I would venture that had he been born to a wealthy establishment family, such as the Bush or Kennedy clans, Charlie would have been President of the United States long before now.

Charlie Keating, with little going for him in the beginning, learned quickly how to exploit every personal asset, including some that were more fiction than fact. His one major real asset, the seemingly unquenchable desire to reach the top and to be "somebody," served as the catalyst and driving force behind every move he made.

Keating throughout school was known as an organizer, always gathering his friends into teams or clubs for some special purpose—always, of course, with himself as captain or president. This big ego did not exist without a concurrent level of ability, however. He enlisted in the Navy at the age of seventeen and rose to become a Navy pilot (shades of George Bush!). At the University of Cincinnati, before graduating with a law degree, he was an all-American on the swim team.

Charlie and his law partner moved quickly into the world of big-business wheeling and dealing, when they, early on, represented Carl Lindner. Lindner was a pioneer in the art of the leveraged deal and the corporate takeover before such transactions became a popular part of the financial scene. This is when the young lawyer learned that big things could be accomplished in the business world without the necessity of using one's own money. During this learning experience he also picked up a good working knowledge of the inside world of politics, as he helped his younger brother Bill win—first, a city council seat in Cincinnati, and later two terms in the U.S. Congress. Charlie was now poised for the big time, and had a pretty firm idea where he wanted to go and how to get there. He managed to acquire the American Continental Corporation, a company spun off from the holdings of his mentor, Lindner, and moved his base of operations to Phoenix, Arizona.

About this time, I first met Charles Keating, Jr., as he joined the small, obscure Cat Cay Club on a miniature Bahamian island just sixty miles east of Miami, Florida. It was there that he would find a fertile greenhouse for his social and business ambitions, and the club that dominated the island's existence would provide rich fodder for Keating's form of ego gratification.

Charlie and his family took a liking to the tropical island and Charlie planned on building a small vacation hideaway on its warm shore. Although I'm sure his intention at the time was no more than to acquire a small place where he could escape the frenetic pace of the business world, this was not to be, as the ever-present ego drive took over.

Formed as an openly snobbish enclave for the "right" kind of people, the Cat Cay Club attracted members who aspired to emulate the exclusivity of legendary Palm Beach, Florida. It had been an exclusive vacation spot and hideaway for rich establishment and political types, but had sunk into disuse and decay during the 60s. W.F. (Al) Rockwell, Jr., Chairman of the gigantic Rockwell International Corporation, along with some of his social and business buddies, had recently taken on the task of breathing some life into the moribund island. Using the political (both U.S. and Bahamian) and financial power of his defense-oriented conglomerate, Al Rockwell had the club up and running again by the time Charlie Keating arrived on the scene. Given to frequent "black tie" and social gatherings in their tropical hideaway, club members lived for those occasions when they could rub shoulders with the social elite. Al Rockwell ruled triumphantly over his doting court, since members of the club were given ample opportunity to mingle with the defense contractor's frequent guests from the show business centers of Hollywood and the U.S. Senate.

There immediately ensued an almost classic war of egos between the privileged inheritor of wealth and position, Rockwell, and the outsider, Keating, who made no effort to disguise his contempt for the Rockwell Corporation's chairman.

As Charlie began construction on his planned simple vacation retreat, Al undertook a major addition to his home on the island which was to make it the largest of the twenty or thirty then existing. Charlie, already campaigning behind the scenes to supplant Al as Number One on the island paradise, abruptly canceled plans for his "cottage" and brought in one of his Arizona architects to design a home befitting his self-perceived superior stature. The end result was a large, flamboyant mansion, dwarfing anything else then existing on the island. Score one up for Charlie!

Not to be outdone by this arrogant interloper, Al had his company develop a massive entertainment complex containing quarters and dining facilities for thirty, a private marina with several fishing yachts, swimming pool, tennis courts, and long stretches of lush ocean beaches on both sides of the tiny island. No question now, the momentum had shifted, advantage Rockwell! Charlie, at that stage of his career, couldn't match the financial muscle of the huge Rockwell International Corporation, and temporarily faded into the background.

The Rockwell complex, costing that prime U.S. defense contractor over $10 million to develop, was (for accounting purposes) buried in one of their subsidiary companies that existed for the sole purpose of providing facilities to entertain important guests of the parent company. Al Rockwell, as chairman of the corporation that existed largely on U.S. Government defense and space contracts, ruled regally over many lavish parties held in this tropical hideaway. Far from the public, and the scrutiny of the press, big names from the Washington political scene were paraded in and out to enjoy the luxurious life-style and to pay proper homage to King Al. Former Texas Senator John Tower, when he headed the powerful Senate Defense Committee, was almost a permanent resident at the complex.

For Keating, Cat Cay was a happy hunting ground made to order for political, business, and social self-promotion. Even though unable to displace Rockwell as the island's social leader, Charlie's place was none the less desirable for those seeking a throne at which to pay homage.

Charlie created a fictional persona, to go with his naturally outgoing personality, without ever actually presenting false credentials. Although never progressing beyond initial Navy pilot training during World War II, the impression was created that he had been a combat fighter-pilot and war hero. Similarly, although a star swimmer in college and named to an all-American team, his aquatic accomplishments became legend in the minds of many of his Cat Cay Club members. I recall one of those awestruck expatriates telling me, "He was an Olympic Gold Medal winner, you know."

Not one to let an opportunity slide, Charlie established an annual social affair on the island, known officially as the Cat Cay Olympics, but generally referred to as "Charlie's Games." With his acknowledged organizational and persuasive powers, he had grown members enthusiastically vying for prizes in such demanding athletic pursuits as egg throwing and three-legged races. The high point of these parties, run by the entire Keating family, was the thrill when the host bestowed, with appropriate flattering speeches, awards to the winners. Colorful caps advertising Charlie's island home, "Bongo Bay," and "Charlie's Olympics" T-shirts, were provided for all lucky enough to be invited to participate.

Invitation to and participation in Keating's island high jinks led to the ultimate reward, an evening party at Charlie's spectacular home overlooking the Atlantic Ocean. With its two-story glass walls and multilevel patios overlooking the tropical moonlit beach, the tall, craggy promoter played the gracious host, adoringly surrounded by his substantial family.

Charlie gave the socially ego-driven club members the stroking and attention they so avidly sought, but not without extracting his price. Never forgetting his major goal, being the salesman he was, he knew he had his captive audience in the palm of his hand. No one got away without learning, personally and privately, from their host that he was making the opportunity of a lifetime available to them. It was thus that many of the self-considered sophisticated members of this exclusive island club ended up just as badly burned as those other, less affluent investors suckered by his Lincoln Savings promoters!

This ability of Keating to win support for his ventures by appealing to the character weaknesses present in most individuals stood him in good stead when he seduced the senators who are now infamous as the Keating Five. As to them, their egos well cared for by their positions, he recognized and exploited their insatiable greed to accomplish the same goals. Cat Cay had been fun and games, but here was the ultimate conquest!

Returning now to Al Rockwell: the flaunting of his power on Cat Cay and the obsequious behavior of the Washington power structure—these were more than Charlie could stomach. Jealous of the attention showered on Al by his important guests, Charlie Keating pointedly avoided all social affairs on the island where the pompous Rockwell held sway.

One episode illustrating the petty level to which these two colossal egos had sunk took place at a meeting of the Cat Cay Club's board of directors. Charlie, a board member and still trying to establish dominance, invited the entire board to hold a regular meeting at his country club resort in Arizona. Continuing his campaign to become Number One, Charlie pulled out all the stops to house and entertain his guests. Alas, despite his best efforts, Al, still carrying the big corporate clout, did it to him again! On the last day of the meeting, a Boeing 727 jetliner swooped low over the clubhouse, rattling rafters and sending all the members outside to see what was happening. As the giant aircraft banked sharply over the golf course for another pass, Al, with a smirk, turned to Charlie and casually remarked "Oh, I guess that's my plane coming to take me back to Pittsburgh." Charlie, who should have known Al used these corporate jets all the time for his personal travel, for once was speechless at this master putdown!

This often childish warfare between the slow-thinking beneficiary of a fantastically successful father and the ambitious, driving outsider from Cincinnati continued for a number of years. In his own mind, Charlie felt that logically it should have been he who had the silver spoon in his mouth. Later, as we'll see, there was to be an ironic twist to this tug-of-war between the two.

During my occasional association with Keating on the island, and with current developments in his career, I began to realize what a truly complex life he developed from a basically simple personality. His ego had been so overpowering that to most observers nothing else was visible. Charlie cannot participate in anything—social, business, or casual sport—unless he is the focus of attention. His philosophy, once espoused by Vince Lombardi, is that "Winning isn't everything, it's the *only* thing." This force in his being causes most to merely write him off as being ruthlessly ambitious. Sadly, underneath this flamboyant, pushy exterior, there is still the small boy trying desperately to be liked. This was again brought home to me one day recently when I received in the mail a videotape from Charlie's public relations office. The tape is comprised of a number of TV appearances by Keating on such programs as CNN's "Moneyline," NBC's "Meet the Press," CNN's "Crossfire," and ABC's "Good Morning America." Obviously, Keating felt the programs showed him in a good light, whereas most observers, I am sure, would squirm in embarrassment watching the interviewers attacking him for his actions as head of the failed Lincoln Savings.

Keating's life, by most standards, would have to be considered bizarre. The contrasts in his public and private behavior make for good copy, but illuminate little of what is really there. Early in his years on Cat Cay, he acquired an ocean-racing powerboat, all smoking engines and incredible noise. His announced intention was to use the boat to commute between Miami and the island at better than fifty miles per hour! He made only a few trips in this high-powered bomb, finding that sore kidneys were a high price to pay, considering that he did not draw the attention he desired. Instead of marveling at his derring-do, the other members sat on the decks of their eighty-foot yachts and wondered about his sanity. That roughneck caper stood in marked contrast to his regular habit of having fresh roses shipped to the island so his maids could lay one on his pillow every night before he retired. These strange contrasts are coming more to light as the news media probe the background of this newly spotlighted personality. His close relationship to his family, who all live adjacent to his home in a complex at one of his developments, and his long-time campaigning against pornography are revealed. He has supported good causes, such as his long-time underwriting of the work of Mother Theresa. Once, in a combination showbiz-religious display, he flew a priest to Phoenix where he joined over 500 guests in a mass recitation of the Rosary in the ballroom of one of his hotels. Contrast this with the apparent indifference with which he allowed his Lincoln Savings to stiff thousands of poor investors with worthless bonds from his company.

Charlie, a born salesman, is always "on" but despite his forceful personality, he was not very successful in raising the money for his grandiose plans in Arizona. Even among those who liked him, the common word among his acquaintances was "Don't ever invest anything with Charlie Keating!"

With plans beyond the reach of his organization, and remembering his early training under Carl Lindner, it was inevitable that Charlie would gravitate toward the swinging big-timers of Wall Street. This, and his knowledge on how to get and use political clout, bring us to the real horror of the "Keating Five."

Chapter 7
Charlie Knows Politics

If anyone needed an example of the crass sellout of our government by corrupted leaders, they could certainly make a solid case out of the politically connected life of one man, Charles H. Keating, Jr. There are many others, of course, and we'll take a look at some of them, but for sheer arrogance on the briber's side and groveling avarice on the bribee's, Charlie's story tells it all!

Starting with his early exposure to the political process in the campaigns of his younger brother, Keating stayed close to the seats of power, whether at the local, state, or federal level. He never missed an opportunity to make a lasting contact—not very difficult when you note his lavish expenditures to set up those contacts. Once he bought his connection, he fully expected—and demanded—that it pay off quickly and tangibly.

When asked by a reporter whether his generous financial support and favors in any way influenced political figures to take up his cause in such cases as his fight against federal regulators who were attempting to curtail his wheeling and dealing at Lincoln Federal, Charlie replied, "I want to say, in the most forceful way I can, I certainly hope so!"

Knowing Charlie, I can say this public statement was no slip of the tongue: He truly believed that he had paid for a service, and by his standards he was entitled to receive his money's worth. It would not enter his mind that maybe his attempt to buy influence was wrong, per se. In the convoluted standards of people like Keating, what they want is, by definition, right, and they quickly become indignant when they feel they are not getting everything they paid for. One thing my experience with Charlie has indicated:

You can always expect him to "tell it like it is" because that is the way he thinks it should be! This characteristic should make the ongoing congressional and court hearings interesting to follow—but I digress by getting ahead of the story.

Charlie's overpowering ego made it hard for him to exert political power quietly behind the scenes. One friend remarked that Keating desperately needed to be liked. In my opinion, it was more that he wanted people to know how important and powerful he was. No faceless insider position for him! Early in his attempts at a public career, he was appointed by President Nixon to a study commission on the effects of pornography on the country. True to his now well-recognized desire for the limelight, he held up the final report of the full commission so he could present his own individual report. His strong antipornography position coming from the study was to become a keystone in his public life, as he became a vocal crusader and financial supporter of causes opposed to moral degeneration (not to be confused with the immorality of bribery, of course).

Some of his political adventures were amusing, but quite indicative of his self-centered desire for recognition. This egocentric flaw in his character did him in when he assumed the position of campaign treasurer in former Texas Governor John Connally's bid for the presidential nomination of the Republican Party in 1980. During that campaign, Charlie was responsible for accommodation arrangements for Connally's personal appearances out in the hustings. At one major affair in California, Charlie booked the candidate into a standard hotel room while he himself occupied the executive suite on the top floor! Keating was summarily fired from the campaign, quite unable to understand the indignation of the big Texan that he considered himself more important than the man he was working for.

Undaunted by his rebuff during the campaign, Charlie showed up at the Republican nominating convention that year in Detroit. He roamed the halls and hotels, closely followed by one of his hired hands from the Cat Cay, Bahamas, operation. This dutiful "gopher," with camera at the ready, was assigned the task of photographing Keating every time he got anywhere near anyone remotely politically important. These intimate little scenes were always valuable when trying to impress someone, or to swing a deal later.

After Ronald Reagan was elected president in 1980, Keating immediately filed application to become United States ambassador to the Bahamas. Still smarting from Al Rockwell's regular besting of him on the island, Charlie felt he could accomplish the ultimate putdown by arriving in that prestigious position. So sure was he that his mere asking would make it so, he announced to friends in the Bahamas that the appointment was set. On one visit to Cat Cay, he boasted, "I can't wait to see that SOB's (Rockwell's) face when I set down in my government helicopter and personal U.S. marine guards!"

Alas, Charlie was not to win that final Rockwell skirmish, either. Keating's checkered past rose up to kill the appointment before it got beyond early consideration. The routine FBI check given all potential presidential appointments canceled any further chance of Charlie getting a government position. In 1979, Keating and his mentor, Lindner, had been accused of fraud in diverting $14 million in assets from the company they operated in Ohio. The two financial wheeler-dealers signed a consent decree, under which Lindner agreed to return $1.4 million to the company. There is plenty of room to speculate, at this point, why that type of background was ignored when federal regulators okayed Charlie's takeover of Lincoln Federal in California. That move by Keating, clearly unallowable in light of his record in Ohio, nonetheless breezed through, and positioned Keating to become one of the preeminent political and financial swingers of our time.

After the government blessing was said over Charlie's move into the big leagues of influence, he turned, naturally, to another big swinger to finance the deal. True to character, Keating turned to junk bonds to finance his takeover of Lincoln, engineered by none other than the infamous Michael Milken of Drexel-Burnham-Lambert. Please note that both Drexel and Keating are now in bankruptcy—but not before the horse was stolen out of the barn and many innocent people were financially ruined.

Okay, so now we have Charlie sitting atop a massive, if wobbly, financial pyramid. How did he do that? Considering his record up to Lincoln Federal, his rise was not the sort of thing Horatio Alger would have held up to praise. Actually, Keating's apparent success to this point is about as incongruous as the specter of Willie Sutton, the fabled bank robber, suddenly appearing as chairman of the Federal Reserve Board!

Where there's a will, however, there's a way. There's little doubt that Charlie had the will, and our government leaders, at high levels indeed, were panting to present him with a way! I remember a somewhat shady character a number of years ago in Chicago expounding on the Mafia philosophy toward government and politics. As we discussed the fact that organized crime functioned effectively only where government law enforcement was either corrupt or deliberately indifferent toward their activities, I asked why the Mafia didn't enter into politics openly to elect their own people. He laughed and said "We don't have to elect our own people, that gets to be too expensive. We just wait until the voters make their choice and then we buy him!"

At the time, as a somewhat younger idealist, I was shocked that anyone could hold such a callous opinion of our elected leaders. But as time has gone by, I've found that the system is far worse off than he had indicated. It is only because so many of the politically powerful in our government can be "had," that the Charlie Keatings can achieve their pinnacles virtually unmolested.

Charlie instinctively knew that everyone has a "hot button." He also knew that these personality or character twists were mostly in areas that the individuals would rather not publicize.

By learning of and making use of these flaws, it is possible to gain effective control over the life of the individual. The swinging government world of Washington doesn't necessarily contain more hot buttons than the rest of the country, but because of the unusual power held by this secluded society they are more readily reached. Former Senator Gary Hart's hot button was intimate relationships with the opposite gender, and it became his downfall. Congressman Barney Frank's button, on the other hand, was the same gender, and the House of Representatives voted to reprimand him. But of all the areas where individuals can be swayed, the most dominant, not unexpectedly, is money.

If you subscribe to the idea that "the love of money is the root of all evil," then the task of seeking the hot button becomes far simpler. Use the money to gain the edge, and then let the individual apply it to whatever excess he wishes. Now we're back to the basic rule of marketing: Find the demand, fill the need. From top to bottom of our political system, the demand for money is paramount. In our freewheeling economy, the money supply seems endless; thus the market is formed.

Once Charlie got his hands on Lincoln Federal, his cash flow, once in the respectable range of seven figures, now reached the heady eight and nine figures. It didn't take long for the system to note Charlie was racing before brisk financial winds, and those with the power to sell were quick to hoist their own sails in his wake. Keating and his associates, long accustomed to playing the system at the lower level to gain their ends, now could look beyond county commissioners and even minor congressmen: the big leagues of the U.S. Senate beckoned.

Charlie Keating has garnered reams of publicity over his big deals with the "Keating Five," but it took more than those five grasping senators to get him where he is. Early on, he had found that the most useful hot button was the campaign fund. Here was an area with great opportunity to pass on money to important people without technically violating any laws. Remember, we're talking about officeholders who cut their political teeth in the early political party training where the rule was, "First, get the money." For those unversed in the political system, "campaign funds" are thought of as money raised and spent solely for the purpose of electing someone to office. That these are, in reality, personal slush funds for the candidates is not generally known. Not only are millions of dollars in campaign money converted for personal use, but under our laws most of the conversion is legal! We'll go into detail a little later, but for now it's sufficient to recognize the drive behind acquiring the money for those giant slush funds.

As an example of the prominence of these campaign pots in the system, we can draw another item from the Keating file, In Arizona, a few years ago, Keating and his associates contributed over $55,000 out of a total campaign fund of $58,000 accumulated by that state's attorney general, Bob Corbin. The interesting factors here were that Mr. Corbin was running for office unopposed and needed no election funds, plus—surprise—this chief law officer of the state never was able to find anything irregular with any of Keating's questionable dealings in Arizona. This means of funneling funds, legally, to favorable officials is not at all unusual. I'm sure many of you can recall examples, particularly of congressmen, where large campaign funds were accumulated for nonexistent or token election races.

In the area of campaign contributions alone, Keating and his closely controlled employees in recent years contributed over $2 million! That's just what can be traced through skimpy and inaccurate campaign reports filed by elected officials. Besides the loopholes allowing large amounts to slide through campaigns, there is an awful lot of money being lavished on elected officials in other, unreported, areas. Since Charlie makes such an enticing subject, and certainly was no piker in his purchase of power, we'll continue with him as one of our prime examples of the rot in our system.

Chapter 8
Normal Constituent Service!

As the harsh and critical light of public scrutiny has shone over the cringing "Keating Five," those esteemed senators have firmly maintained that they were merely performing "normal constituent service" in their efforts to protect and cover up the activities of their mentor. In this position they have been loyally supported by their colleagues in Washington's most exclusive club, who indicate they, too, would have gone to bat in the same manner for one of their valued constituents. So let's move on with our close look at Charles H. Keating, Jr., and see just how normal a constituent he was to this diverse group of national leaders.

One thing that the evidence will reveal—Charlie Keating knew full well the risk he was taking in his highly leveraged wheeling and dealing from the very start. Despite any defense he may mount to justify his actions, his moves on the political side smack very much of a desire to "cover his bets." Had his takeover and operation of Lincoln Federal followed the path of normal business practices, his expenditure of millions of dollars to cover his political tail would have been unnecessary. That he accelerated his purchase of influence in Washington at the very start of his venture is a pretty good indication that Charlie knew he was not moving into a pure white, virgin territory!

Earlier, when Keating was only operating in the million-dollar league of land development, before his plunge into the big leagues of finance, he showed an astute grasp of the importance of political clout in his ventures. Not to be nitpicking, since it is probably just another one of those frequent coincidences we find in these cases involving government oversight, consider Charlie's hometown. In 1980, Keating and friends kicked in over $120,000 toward the election campaigns for the Phoenix, Arizona, city council. Cruel finger pointers in the community are quick to draw attention to the fact that Charlie and his cohorts never lost a zoning request that came before those democratically elected representatives of the people. After batting one thousand at the local level, it was natural that Charlie should use the same swing in the big leagues.

In review, to make sure we have the sequence in its proper perspective, here's the setup. Charlie's vast development and land speculation operations in Arizona, mostly through American Continental Corporation, were always teetering on the edge of financial overreach. The land speculator's best friend—his god—is his banker. Without a liberal source of borrowed money in that leveraged business, you're apt to be left dead in the desert sands.

Charlie tried to raise money on his own by selling bonds in his company. That method didn't work, as his company was too thin financially to attract the size of investment he needed. What else, then, but to get his own bank? Lincoln Federal in Irvine, California, was vulnerable to a takeover and Charlie launched a successful campaign to acquire it. Still unable to obtain legitimate financing through his Arizona company, he turned to Drexel-Burnham-Lambert for a junk bond issue. In the nifty way these things are done, Lincoln Federal bought the bonds to provide the funds Charlie needed to take it over!

Now Charlie was in the big time, but he needed to deploy defensive forces to protect his flanks. Our willing senators were panting in the wings, ready and willing to become Charlie's defensive Green Berets.

Now, about those "constituent services." Let us make sure our terminology is clear and accurate before moving on. For that, we turn to the *American Heritage Dictionary:*

Con-stit-u-ent, noun

1. someone represented by another: client
2. someone represented by an elected official

Okay, we can buy that; Charlie (as we'll see) funneled enough money and favors to his Five that he certainly seems qualified under the first definition as a (paying!) client. It also seems he fits well under definition number two, as far as the two senators from his home state of Arizona are concerned. For the sake of argument, you could extend that one by considering Charlie's business operations as quasi-people, so Lincoln Federal in California, the Hotel Ponchartrain in Detroit, and his business and family roots in Cincinnati would make the connection with the senators from California, Michigan, and Ohio. So, Your Honor, we rest our case, constituency has been established. Now we are free to address the subject of whether these were "normal" constituent services, as provided by the distinguished leaders of our republic.

Let's first look at the experienced squad leader of the Five, Senator Dennis DeConcini of Arizona. As senior senator from Charlie's home state, he naturally stepped forward to take command of the operation on behalf of his "constituent." It was he who convened the private meeting of his distinguished club members of the Keating Five. That historic meeting had no purpose other than to warn the federal bureaucrats to "bug off" in the continuing investigation of their good friend Charlie. Details of that high-level gathering have been well documented in the media, and will probably merit further attention in some pending court actions. Our mission today is to examine how this one constituent could bring these powerful Senate leaders together so forcefully on his behalf. If there are other constituents who could accomplish such a feat, I'd appreciate hearing from them.

But, on with Dennis. How could he, of all people, allow himself to be drawn into such a situation? Before we go on, though, let me remind you of that great and original dictum laid down by the earliest political trainers: Get the money.

Senator DeConcini officially received only $55,000 (this stuff must be getting to me—how can $55,000 be "only"?) from Charlie Keating and friends toward his election campaign. Even this amount—chicken feed by Washington standards—was later returned by the good senator in an apparent attempt to expiate his sins. So why do we pick on him? As we promised to elaborate upon later, campaign funds only represent the smallest tip of the iceberg of the money expended to purchase our government.

Into the scene come Ron Ober and Earl Katz, two of the closest advisers and campaign handlers of Senator DeConcini. Again, in one of those constant coincidences, these two gentlemen from the senator's inner circle received over $50 million in loans from Keating's Lincoln Federal. Over $30 million of that was unsecured! The distinguished senator protests repeatedly that he knew nothing of this highly unusual financing obtained by his cohorts from good old Charlie. Even though these loans were so risky they had to be extended and enlarged several times over three years (an extremely friendly accommodation by "constituent" Keating), the Dennis insists he did not know anything about them.

The senator's continued insistence he knew nothing about the actions of his closest advisers is at least consistent with his apparent lack of knowledge about Charlie himself. The news media in Arizona—not the hardest state in the union to stay on top of—had been chronicling the saga of Keating's affairs for several years. You would think that someone on the senator's staff would have taken note of the headlines concerning Charlie's state tax problems and apparent undue influence over certain state officials, and taken it upon themselves to warn the Dennis to stay away from Keating. Yet, despite the evidence under his very nose, Senator Dennis DeConcini plowed ahead and got caught up in the mess. On balance, I would have to say Senator DeConcini is a worthy member of the Keating Five!

Also in Arizona, Senator John McCain found Charlie to be an important "constituent" and became a willing member of the Five. Senator McCain received over $112,000 from Keating and friends toward his election campaign fund. Unlike the Dennis, however, John kept his. With the junior senator from Arizona, Charlie found a different hot button than the huge staff loans lavished on his compatriot.

Enter now the Bahamas connection. Apparently Senator McCain and his family, after being exposed to Charlie's gracious hospitality at the Cat Cay retreat, became frequent travelers to that lush tropical hideaway.

At this point, I must exercise author's privilege to bring you an update on the long-running duel between Charlie and his nemesis, Al Rockwell. Since we last visited this saga, a palace uprising at the Rockwell International Corporation resulted in W.F. (Al) Rockwell, Jr., being ousted from the board of directors of the company his father had founded. Once Charlie got wind of Al's demise as king of the island, he moved quickly to cement relations with the corporation. The result was that now Charlie and that giant defense contractor began to use their neighboring properties on Cat Cay in the Bahamas jointly to their mutual advantage. Since the Rockwell Corporation and Charlie both frequently entertained influential political guests, and sometimes one or the other would need more space, they combined properties for entertainment purposes. Finally, Charlie had gone one-up on Al!

Back to the junior senator from Arizona, who had become such a frequent guest of the semi-joint Keating-Rockwell private enclave in the tropics. When the unpleasant publicity concerning the Five surfaced, along with the stories of his many vacations at Charlie's place, Senator McCain sheepishly repaid over $13,000 in air fares paid by Charlie to get him there. Unmentioned was the considerable cost of housing and entertaining him and his family on the island. That this was not a minuscule sum is indicated by the fact that the Rockwell Corporation, which kept meticulous records on their operation, calculated that it took in excess of a thousand dollars a person per three-day visit to entertain properly on the island. Senator McCain, like Arizona's senior senator, apparently had not noticed any of Keating's prior problems in the state of Arizona. Although not as well known as the Dennis, he is nonetheless a worthy addition to the Five!

Moving cross-country for the next mod-squad member, the spotlight shines on Senator Donald Riegle. This pious one benefitted from over $76,000 in contributions from Charlie. It was not hard to whip up nice fundraisers for the senator from Michigan, since Keating and his friends had purchased the Ponchartrain Hotel in Detroit. When the storm broke over the Keating affair, Senator Riegle (an important ally as Senate Banking Committee chairman) performed the popular ablution of those caught with their hands in the cookie jar by returning the money. But then Senator Riegle compounded his problem by insisting, "At no time did I initiate any contact with regulators concerning Lincoln."

Unfortunately for the credibility of the distinguished senator from Michigan, it shortly came out that the Donald had met privately with a Lincoln Federal auditor and its general counsel in 1987 (coincidentally the same year he got the 76 grand). Shortly after that private confab, he suggested a senatorial meeting about Lincoln with the top U.S. savings and loan regulator!

Although not as visible as some of the other, more outstanding members of the Five, on deviousness alone Senator Riegle is certainly qualified to hold his honored position on the squad.

With the fourth member of the Keating bunch, we begin to see the real benefits in sitting near the centers of power in Washington and knowing how to turn such position into tangible benefits. Senator John Glenn of Ohio, former astronaut, former presidential candidate, and current close friend of Charlie Keating, parlayed his connections into over $230,000 of the Keating loot and, like the Dennis, the benefits of association with Charlie extended beyond those substantial direct dollars, as three of Glenn's close associates, including his presidential campaign manager (although I find it hard to understand why he should have been rewarded) became lobbyists on the Keating payroll.

Here again, with the astronaut-senator, one has to wonder about the myopia of his substantial staff. Like the Dennis, certainly Glenn should have been well aware of the Charlie Keating background—all the more since Charlie started his checkered career in Ohio, and it was in Ohio after a lengthy investigation by the Federal Securities and Exchange Commission that Charlie was charged with fraud and ultimately signed a consent decree when his Ohio partner paid back $1.4 million of the misappropriated funds. As senator from that great state, you would think that John Glenn or his staff would have seen storm warnings whenever the Keating name came up. Maybe the warning flags were just hard to see through the haze of the almost quarter-million dollars and the lucrative Keating jobs for his associates.

A little later we'll be getting into the fun and games of private foundations and PACs (Political Action Committees) such as Senator Glenn and others had available to receive big gobs of money from guys like Charlie. At least for now, there is definitely a good case for inclusion of the distinguished senator from Ohio to Gold Card membership in the Keating Five!

Now back to California, which, lest you forget, is the home of the oft-mentioned Lincoln Federal Savings. It was from this state of movie fiction, dancing raisins, and funny parades in San Francisco, that Charlie was to find his greatest supporter. Senator Alan Cranston, most noted for his expensive campaigns and strident liberal philosophy, was especially valuable in Washington because of his standing in the Senate's archaic seniority system. Charlie, never one to miss such important details, pulled out all the stops to make sure the cadaverous (a description coined by popular radio host Rush Limbaugh) senator was solidly in his corner as he battled federal regulators trying to rein in his rape of Lincoln's depositors.

Senator Cranston received a mere $40,000 (I hate myself for belittling such a sum) from Keating toward his election campaign. But the wily Californian had something else going for him on the side—a private foundation supposedly set up for the altruistic purpose of encouraging laggard citizens to register as voters. Charlie, never one to miss an opportunity, generously donated over $850,000 (now, that's close enough to a million that it can't be belittled) to Cranston's charity. As with the wonders of PACs which we promised to cover in detail later, the glories of these private foundations will get our full attention. For now, though, we should elaborate a little on Senator Cranston's private game room.

Senator Cranston's private foundation just happens to be run by his son Kim, presumably at a livable salary. The purpose of this tax-exempt business is to coax nonvoters into registering and becoming full-fledged, concerned citizens. For years, picky Republican Party officials (the senator is a Democrat) have complained that this nonpartisan foundation seemed more intent on registering Democrats than Republicans. This, of course, would be a violation of federal law, and at this writing the FBI and the Internal Revenue Service are reported to be conducting investigations into Senator Cranston's (and his son's) private operation.

It goes without question that Senator Alan Cranston of California is a well-qualified member of the Keating Five!

At the present writing, Charles Keating, Jr., is facing dates in court, both civil and criminal, concerning his operation of the government-seized Lincoln Federal and the bankrupt American Continental Corporation. The U.S. Senate Committee on Ethics is also "looking at" actions of the Keating Five. If this subdivision of that distinguished private club follows true to form, we can confidently expect a mild reprimand, or at worst, ten lashes with a wet noodle!

So that we don't depart the subject of Charles Keating, Jr., thinking that his only attempt at buying influence in Washington was through the Five, ponder on these little details: In the recorded donation filings with the Federal Elections Commission in Washington, a highly unreliable source for complete reports, as we'll establish later, you can find nearly half a million dollars of donations from Charlie. The recipients of this largess read like a "Who's Who" in government.

Names showing up as being supported by Keating's generosity include: Senators Wilson, Wirth, Mattingly, Armstrong, Dole, and Hecht; and Congressmen Kolbe, Pashayan, Kyl, Barnard, Rhodes, Kemp, Annunzio, Stump, Dornan, Neal, and Hubbard.

The Republican Party also received generous donations from Charlie's gang. However, although Charlie supported many Democratic officeholders of influence, I can find no indication he gave anything to the Democrat Party.

These direct donations to political officeholders will only tell a small portion of the story of the buying of Washington. There are literally more ways than you can count to bestow favors on the politically powerful for their help.

One universal characteristic of monetary lust as exhibited by the grasping political contacts of Charlie Keating is that the point of ultimate satisfaction can never be reached. Charlie, the quintessential manipulator, knows that such individuals are incapable of taking the money and running—they always hang around for more. Frequently that unsatisfied hunger is what eventually does them in, as they reach too far for their undeserved rewards.

The Keating Five, although already having benefitted substantially from Charlie's millions, were sure there was more where that came from. So when Charlie called for action to save his crumbling empire, the greedy senators dutifully met to throw their considerable power behind the "Save Charlie Keating" gambit. They figured there were more big bucks where the original came from, and correctly figured Charlie would be perfectly willing to pay for continuing services rendered. Whether it was social, political, or business, Charlie certainly knew how to get to the heart of the subject!

As a final line one of those areas devoted to the blessing of politicians, in all the travails of Charlie Keating, and the closing of his businesses, he no longer owns the lush retreat on Cat Cay in the Bahamas. Also, the Rockwell International Corporation has disposed of its resort on the same island. As of this moment, both places are sitting quietly under the tropic sun, as exotic greenery spreads over their once carefully tended grounds and the private harbor, once bustling with celebrity-loaded deep-sea fishing yachts, gradually fills with drifting sand.

Chapter 9
There Oughta Be a Law

It would be difficult to find any subject in politics where everyone involved, no matter what their philosophical leaning, would be in full agreement. The present-day means of campaign financing, however, come as close to receiving unanimous condemnation as anything since we declared war on Japan in 1941. Pick up any newsmagazine or paper today and chances are you'll find some article chronicling the whining complaints of a congressman or senator about all the time they must devote to raising money for their next campaign. It is absolutely accepted that fund-raising for the next election starts the day after the current election. If you want to subject yourself to at least an hour of really confusing rhetoric, ask your favorite Washington leader, "What do you think of our campaign financing system?"

Despite the myriad reasons you'll hear as to why the present system is bad, and despite the very few expressions of support, take note of how many years the election codes have remained unchanged. You would think that when virtually all the principals charged with writing the laws find a series of laws abhorrent, there would be a high priority given to making some changes. Could it be that the present setup is so beneficial to those holding office that merely "reading their lips" doesn't tell the true story?

The evils and dangerous temptations created by huge cash transactions in politics are no less a problem than that created by the big money in crime and drugs. The level of public and official complaints in both areas rival each other for our attention and action. The uniqueness on the political side, however, is that the loudest calls for action come from the participants who are also the biggest beneficiaries of the status quo!

But, you say, why don't we crack down on the abuses in campaign funding, let's declare war! Our government leaders are quick to jump on bandwagons for the periodic wars against crime, and the current headline-grabbing war against drugs—why not a war against campaign corruption? Discuss this subject with the average law-abiding citizen and you will usually draw the retort, "There ought to be a law!"

Well, surprise, surprise, not only is there already a law, there are literally hundreds of them! Let's look at those campaign laws currently on the books, not only at the federal level, but in all fifty states plus other jurisdictions.

So you shouldn't labor under the misapprehension that this subject has been neglected by our lawmakers in Washington, the current Federal Election Code and ancillary acts of Congress require several hundred pages of fine print. Almost any question you care to raise about accepting and expending funds to get elected to Congress or the presidency is answered somewhere within that maze of law! A word of caution is necessary here, as an old insurance agent friend used to warn about insurance policies, "The bold print giveth, but the fine print taketh away," so don't take the code at face value. At the risk of boring you with redundancy, always keep in mind the election campaign laws have all been written by the very political campaigners the code is supposed to regulate. Reflect on the implications in that setup as you consider the effect, had John Dillinger or Machine-Gun Kelly written the criminal code. Of course, that is not to say that our distinguished congressmen or senators would be so crude as to favor their own elections or personal well-being in the way they compose election laws.

Okay, simmer down now, that kind of cynical laughter will hold up our progress through the Federal Election Code!

As would be expected, the election laws, while dealing with matters of eligibility and procedures, are most important for what they say concerning how campaign money is to be received and how it is spent. That area of interest would seem to any rational person to be a relatively simple task. Where should the money be allowed to come from, how much should be allowed, and finally a straightforward requirement that all funds be spent on the election process. I'm sure that's the way you or I would write such a code, were we in those power positions in Washington, and I bet it would only take a few succinct pages to get the job done.

Alas, what is logical or right is seldom what is done in the fuzzy world of our government. Again, your attention is drawn to the fact that the rules for the operation of the asylum are being written by the inmates! If you grant there might be deviousness in their approach, remember that most of the authors and their staffs are lawyers. The end result, while crafted to appear simple on its face, is masterfully complicated by language even a linguist would stumble over. Such complication accomplishes the main goal—keeping curious readers like us from grasping the wonderful loopholes provided by the writers for the sole benefit of those same writers.

First, under contributions, observe this language:

> (A) No person shall make contributions to any candidate . . . for Federal office . . . in the aggregate to exceed $1,000.
> (B) No person shall make contributions to political committees established by a national political party . . . in the aggregate to exceed $20,000.
> (C) No person shall make contributions to any other political committee . . . in the aggregate to exceed $5,000.

That's certainly not hard to understand: they sound like good sensible limitations. But, just a darn minute, go back a few pages and note that our old friend Charlie Keating gave thousands of dollars in excess of these limitations to his "Angels," as well as to many others, not mentioning his generosity to the Republican Party!

The key under this section of the Federal Code is the innocuous singular noun, "person." To comply with this section, while at the same time making sure the personal slush fund of your favorite congressman or senator is well-stocked, you give the limit in your name, then the limit in your spouse's name, then your children, Aunt Mabel, etc. It is not at all unusual for the family dog or pet goldfish to donate the maximum limit as well! The really big influence buyers can expand their horizons of giving by paying special bonuses to their employees who then make nice donations to their favorite politician! So, as I think we can agree, despite all the flowery phrases and seemingly severe restrictions, that portion of the code is meaningless.

Okay, so now we see how our esteemed leaders can accumulate such huge bankrolls in their campaign accounts through the generosity of the "Charlie Keatings" in our system. What personal good is all that money to your favorite spokesman in Washington if they can only spend it on election campaigns? There is an uncomfortably substantial number of our elected leaders who never face any real challenge to their reelection, why do they need those big campaign accounts? "Therein lies the rub," if I may mangle that old English Bard.

Again, let us digest the weighty legal language and get to the heart of the subject of the use of contributed funds.

> Amounts received by a candidate as contributions . . . may be used by such candidate, or individual (Author's comment: This extends the provision of this section to those who are not candidates, i.e., an already elected

> officeholder.) for the purpose of supporting his or her activities to defray any ordinary and necessary expenses incurred with . . . duties as a holder of Federal office . . .

This portion of the code is further expanded as follows:

> . . . (funds) may be used for any other lawful purpose . . . except that . . . any individual who is not a senator or representative . . . to Congress on January 8, 1980 . . . may convert such amounts to personal use other than . . . for ordinary and necessary expenses incurred with . . . duties as a holder of Federal office.

The limitation date in 1980 is significant, as we'll see.

If we were to point a single finger (we do have others to point, however) to illustrate the shame of the sale of our government to the highest bidders, this small section of the election codes would be our target. Reading carefully through all of the Federal Codes, or for that matter, the state codes, pertaining to finances for candidates or political committees, you'll find no real restriction on expenditures. Logic would dictate that election funds should be restricted to elections. A reasonable person, therefore assumes the law clearly declares that those dollars donated towards elections be spent only for those necessities connected with the election process. But logic and, unfortunately, honesty, are not the prime criteria for our elected officials once they get their hands on all that loot!

Once again, note carefully the language, "ordinary and necessary expenses," which, incidentally, is common to most state campaign funding laws. These words are given the broadest possible interpretation by everyone charged with operating the system. Certainly, for example, we all want our elected representatives to maintain a nice appearance, so it is natural that custom-tailored suits and appropriate wardrobes for spouses are found to be "ordinary expenses" for the officeholder's campaign fund. We certainly want our leaders to be alert and well-rested when they approach the arduous task of doing it to us when Congress convenes, so restful vacations become "necessary expenses" from the funds. This whole phase of the ballgame is so attractive, I've known candidates who ran for office just to solicit funds to enhance their style of living. Above all, though, the political system and the media must make sure the poor sucker who mails his $20 donation doesn't really know how it will be used!

Even with all the wondrous possibilities for fun and profit presented by the fat campaign account, the fertile minds of our leaders have been hard pressed to find enough "ordinary and necessary expenses" to use up those pots of gold. After all, you can only wear so many suits, drive so many autos and even vacation time is limited; so a new diversion route was definitely needed. That solution came early in the game as the Washington gang inserted another one of their door opening phrases, "may be used for any other lawful purpose."

Remember, our system of law assumes all acts are lawful unless a statute or court action specifically decrees them unlawful. This sneaky little line, in all the thousands making up the election codes, effectively authorizes the candidates and officeholders to spend their campaign funds for almost any darn thing they want. Of course, it would be a violation of the code to buy a pack of cocaine down at the street corner, because that in itself is unlawful, but it would be perfectly okay to slip the money into your pocket and head out for a glorious night on the town! And that, exactly, is what our leaders in Washington have been doing for years.

For our elected federal officials this wonderful provision in the election law they wrote for themselves has been a multimillion-dollar source of joy. For those who cannot party hard enough to use up the pot at the end of their rainbow, the surplus becomes an additional retirement fund on top of their already lucrative taxpayer-funded pension plan. Because of deliberately misleading reporting, or actual nonreporting, no one knows for sure how much of this kind of money is resting comfortably in the pockets of our Government elite. Occasionally some educated guesses make the news, for example:

> Recently retiring Congressman William Carney (NY) and Eldon Rudd (AZ) took with them over $135,000 of old campaign funds.
> Venerable Congressman Claude Pepper (FL) didn't get to use any of his half-million dollars in campaign funds left when he died in office. His heirs benefitted, however, as it was passed on.
> At this writing, it appears that veteran Congressman Dan Rostenkowski (IL) is one of the leaders of the pack, with over $1 million accumulated in his campaign slush fund!

One of the extra benefits our astute legislative leaders worked into the law allowing them to convert campaign funds to personal use shows the kind of innovation we seldom see in other acts of Congress. Apparently admitting, if only to themselves, that they have not earned this bonanza of extra spending power, they have decreed the money is not taxable! Imagine that, not only do they slip themselves a substantial side income, but the tax man can't touch it! You might want to keep this little deal in mind as you watch Congressman Rostenkowski, Chairman of the powerful House Ways and Means Committee devise new ways to levy federal taxes against your hard-earned income. After he and his cronies stick it to you, they can stuff their loot in their briefcases and take it home untouched.

The personal conversion of campaign funds to retirement bank accounts has drawn enough static from the media (who really wish they had something like it), that Congress was forced to do something about that loophole. It was too good a deal for our sheepish leaders to totally give up, however, so they amended the Code with the 1980 date noted earlier. All this did was to prevent any new members of Congress planning on taking their campaign slush funds with them upon retirement. The good ol' boys who were already there are grandfathered in and can still take it with them. The Senate, apparently lacking the sheer brass of our Congressmen, changed their own rules so none of them can take it with them!

Our leaders, of course, like to point to their small corrections in this personal enrichment program as evidence that they do, indeed have integrity and "the right stuff." They hope, of course, that we, the dull electorate, will not notice that the big loophole allowing their personal use of these funds is still there. The only difference now is that they must spend it all before leaving office, or lose it. Anyone have any doubts that this gang, as good as they are at spending, won't find ways to get rid of the evidence? Vacation homes, anyone?

Chapter 10

Who Minds the Store?

Well, even if the statutes covering election funding are best noted for their generous loopholes, at least we have someone attempting to regulate campaign abuses, right? Remember, our elected leaders in Washington, well aware of the potential for improper usage of those big gobs of money did thoughtfully provide for a Federal Elections Commission to oversee the whole process, right? We're not going to embarrass you by asking if you know what this commission is, and how, or if, it functions!

The Federal Elections Commission is a six-member board, each of whom is appointed by the President of the United States for a six-year term. The providing statute expands at length on the desired credentials for the members chosen for this regulatory body. Boiling it down to simple Washingtonese, they must have good political connections. So that neither of the major political parties may gain the upper hand, the law requires that no more than three of the members may come from one political party, so following the rules of the game the board always has three Republican and three Democrat members. Although members are nominated by the president, the Senate maintains effective control by exercising their approval process. Again, to be sure the two parties remain balanced, if the chairman of the commission is a Republican, the vice chairman must be a Democrat, and vice versa.

If you spend any time around Washington, one thing you learn very quickly is that our power structure does not look kindly upon any "independent" commission whose members show too much independence. Since these boards are made up of citizens who do not spend full-time working at their appointed positions, most of the work and direction of the body is provided by the full-time paid government staff. The staffs for the literally hundreds of commissions and boards come from the huge pool of ambitious young bureaucrats who spend their careers vying for the most lucrative and powerful positions. The best hope for advancement to the top power spots, which are the key staff positions with members of Congress or the Senate and their major committees, is to catch the eye and favor of one of the elected leaders. I think you can catch the drift here: There is little chance for advancement for that lower staff member who arouses the ire of one of the power elite in Congress. Couple this fact of life with the further fact that appointees to these boards have relatively little time to devote to their boards and you begin to understand why policies and agendas germinate within the staff.

Congress, depending upon the degree of control they wish to maintain over their boards, set the personnel and budgets of each commission. Those they would rather not have poking around in areas where they're not wanted get the short end of the stick on funding and the least experienced and influential staffs.

Occasionally there are boards, such as the Federal Elections Commission, that receive enough public attention and approval that the good ol' boys must go to more subtle methods to apply a tight rein on too much independence. With the Federal Elections Commission, that wily old gang on capitol hill made sure they were put on a tight leash.

Congress provided that the Clerk of the House and the Secretary of the Senate sit as ex officio members of the Election Commission. These two very powerful employees of Congress with their large permanent staffs are in prime position to make sure the commission does not do anything to rock the boats of their mentors.

Early in my research into the undue influence of large campaign funds on our national government I ran head on into the laissez faire attitude of the Federal Election Commission toward law enforcement of even the modest provisions of the financing code. The Commission headquarters in Washington devotes its first floor to public access to the computer and microfilm records of campaign and political committee filings. Here you can call up, and make copies if you wish, of any financial report filed under the terms of the law. While scanning annual figures on donations and expenditures of the Republican National Committee, I immediately noted a discrepancy of more than $40 million between the computer summary totals and the copies of final reports from the Committee. When I called this to the attention of the Federal Election Commission floor supervisor then on duty, I was advised, "Oh, that happens all the time, the figures seldom match!"

When I expressed a degree of shock and questioned how such obviously erroneous reports could be allowed to be filed, the FEC staff member, showing disdain at my apparent naivete, replied, "We don't have the time to check on their figures. We just make sure they file their reports on time; whether they're accurate or not is up to them."

Although I have made numerous visits to the FEC office, reviewing what reports they do have on file, I've never quite gotten over the shock of that first visit. It's bad enough to study the federal election laws and find so many glaring loopholes, through which millions of dollars slide through the system, but to cap that with the realization that there are no provisions for audits or even cursory examinations of reports is almost too much to swallow!

Even though the FEC is a sham, insofar as any meaningful enforcement of campaign financing, the two political parties go to great lengths to avoid filing reports on most of their own political funding. Since the federal laws and the FEC have their meager jurisdiction only over funding pertaining to elections for national office, the Republican and Democrat national parties segregate their funds and only file federal reports on those dollars directly pertaining to national elections. The bulk of their money flow is either not reported, or is filed under state election statutes, which make the Federal Election Commission, by comparison, look like a cloistered monastery in strictness. The totally unrecorded funds, which the insiders, for some reason, like to call "soft money," will be covered later.

Considering the gaping loopholes and omissions in the election code, along with the casual attitude towards checking reports, you begin to understand how the Charlie Keatings in our system can so blatantly buy our elected officials. Here, however, a word of caution for those who would venture into the wonderful world of Washington politics. The FEC does have the authority to audit and punish any individual or committee they consider in violation of their reporting standards. Just because they have a cozy symbiotic relationship with the Republican and Democrat national committees, as well as the entrenched power structure in Congress, doesn't mean they don't occasionally make waves! Just try to set up an independent political committee or in any other way attempt to rock the establishment boat and you'll quickly learn about their regulatory powers!

A word here to point out the tremendous influence over permanent government staff employees wielded by elected officials and powerful political party leaders. Although the full-time government employees have job security under the liberal civil service laws, promotions to higher, more rewarding positions come through the political system. Even if you find reasons to question certain activities on the part of the politically elite, such as the Savings and Loan investigators have been finding, or as the FEC employees see every day, you have to be pretty dedicated to cancel your future by blowing the whistle.

Nowhere has the system requirement that you play the game with the politicians been shown more openly than in the recent disgraceful affair causing the resignation of House Speaker Jim Wright of Texas. Among the many other details publicized concerning this wheeler-dealer was an episode illustrating the subject at hand. Wright hired, and promoted to his top staff position, a young man who had been convicted, and remained unrepentant, for a particularly heinous and brutal attempted murder of a young lady store clerk. Although given little publicity at the time, most of Wright's cohorts knew of this individual's background. The good ol' boy code, however, dictated that the political elitists cover for their leader and this staff member of the Speaker of the House of Representatives became one of the most powerful bureaucrats in Congress! Is it any wonder that other permanent government employees, themselves ambitious for advancement, have learned to go along with the political power?

The game of territory consolidation and turf protection shows up in many areas directly involved with the sale of our government. We'll look at some openings for abuse where there isn't even token legislation to protect the citizen's stake in their government. For now, though, let's move on to another of the Federal "regulatory" statutes.

In the early formative years of our new country, government leaders were looked upon as real people, just like us. It's only in recent years that our elected officials have become more media and entertainment idols than leaders. For example, looking back, you could hardly find anyone more "ordinary" than President Ulysses S. Grant. Although a popular and much acclaimed war hero, he never seemed to lose his common touch. It's ironic that this leader from our past should leave as a legacy an institution that bears a large responsibility for the sale of our governing system to special financial interests.

One of Grant's better known human foibles was his propensity toward strong drink. During the Civil War, as a two-fisted military leader under Commander in Chief, President Abe Lincoln, Grant's critics complained to the president about his noted reliance on the bottle. Lincoln's reply, now part of our country's folklore was, "Find out what he's drinking and send a case to all my other generals!" Grant didn't change his ways, but the public elected him president anyway. After spending the early part of the day at those humdrum office tasks usual to the presidency, Grant liked to take an afternoon break away from the White House. His regular practice was to stroll across the White House lawn to the nearby Willard Hotel. Even today, the Willard is a quiet, refined hostelry providing shelter from the helter-skelter of our nation's capital, even though it's not quite as easy for the occupant of the mansion on Pennsylvania Avenue to get there. Entering the lobby of the Willard, Grant would plop himself down in one of their comfortable leather chairs and order a stimulating libation.

The president's daily visitations to the old hotel soon became common knowledge throughout Washington. Politics being what it always has been, those who wanted to catch Grant's ear on a favorite project soon learned to be in or around the Willard lobby at that time of day. Those who waited with patience for the arrival of the old soldier were frequently afforded the opportunity for quiet conversation over drinks they generously bought the nation's leader. Since President Grant had a seemingly unquenchable thirst, and like any drinker worth his salt could hardly refuse to hear what the drink buyer had to say, these enterprising promoters of causes and contracts had their say right at the top level!

Thus was born the practice that since has grown into a massive and not very subtle means of currying favor from government leaders. Today's lobbyists owe their start—even their very name—to the favor seekers who used to wait in the Willard hotel lobby for their contacts. Today, of course, there are not enough hotel lobbies in Washington to hold the more than 20,000 registered lobbyists, not to mention those who are sub rosa! With that kind of territorial saturation, no grasping Washington power figure need look far for the favors available from these smooth operators.

During World War II, with the government's almost insatiable demand for munitions and goods of every description, lobbying exploded into a major Washington industry. To the credit of the United States Congress in those years after the war, they recognized that this type of influence seeking was becoming a serious problem. Our leaders of those days put their heads together and came up with the Federal Lobbying Act of 1946. To their everlasting discredit, however, they came up with a cure that was worse than the disease. In a very short statute (for a Congress usually given to verbosity) they created something that does far more to protect influence buyers than it does to protect the integrity of government. To prove that this slant favorable to lobbyists was not accidental, during the past fifty years every attempt to amend and tighten the lobbying Act of 1946 has been stifled by the inside political leadership in Congress! One thing you can be sure of, anytime our guys in Washington let a regulatory act stand for over half a century, it must be a good deal for them. As for benefiting the establishment politicians, that 1946 Act is a doozy, easily rivaling the Federal Election Code for the goodies it provides.

The Lobbying Act requires that anyone representing another person, company, or organization expending money for the purpose of influencing legislation or the votes of members of Congress must file a report with the Secretary of the Senate or the Clerk of the House. Any expenditure over $10 is considered sufficient to require a report.

This sounded pretty straightforward to me, so I called the Secretary of the U.S. Senate seeking information on our Washington lobbyists. (I hasten to explain, this was during my early, naive period of probing government activities.)

Speaking to a very pleasant young lad in that prestigious office I inquired, "May I have a list of all the lobbyists registered with your office?"

After a somewhat embarrassed pause, the Senate staff member advised, "I'm sorry, we do not keep any list of lobbyists."

"But," I protested, "they are supposed to file with your office."

"Yes, Sir," he replied patiently, "but we only hear from them when they file their spending reports."

Smugly thinking I had now been switched to the right track, I confidently asked, "Okay, then just give me a copy of their financial reports."

"I'm sorry, I can't do that, we don't keep copies."

Beginning to sputter with indignation I demanded, "Just exactly what do you do with those reports, if you don't keep a file?"

"When we get them they're sent over to the Congressional Record for publication in the next edition." Then, trying to be helpful to this obviously misinformed citizen, "You can check back-copies of the Record if you want to see any reports."

By this time I knew how Don Quixote must have felt when the windmills refused to topple after his best charges. Watching my open frustration over what to him seemed a quite logical system (remember he's making a career out of that asylum) he quietly advised, "I'm not supposed to mention this, but there is a publisher in Washington that follows the Lobbying game pretty closely and publishes a book listing all the lobbyists they can find."

Thanking him after he told me the name of the publisher, I took my leave of the office of the Secretary of the United States Senate with a much better understanding of the meaning of obfuscation.

If you are wondering how our government can require registration of lobbyists without keeping a list of those reporting, stay tuned, it gets even better as we move along. You must first understand the sophisticated ways of our lawmakers, who long before we were born had already mastered the art of saying one thing but enacting another. It has long been accepted that lobbyists plying their trade in Washington must register with the Federal Government. This presumption is so common that politicians and media alike always refer to these individuals and organizations as "registered" lobbyists.

The simple truth is, there is no law requiring that lobbyists register! The Act in question never uses the term "register" or any of its derivatives! The Lobbying Act refers only to "regulating" lobbyists by requiring that they report their expenditures to the proper office in Congress. No expenditures, no reports, and no names on file! Like the election Commission, rather than a toothless tiger, this one is a gummed pussycat!

Back to the unofficial list published by Columbia Books in Washington, containing over 22,000 names they've been able to verify. You would think with that many people trying to influence the votes of a few hundred members of Congress, they could inflict bodily injury upon each other, even if they split off into teams of only fifty or so for each Congressman and Senator! If they were buying drinks and food like the ones who used to work over President Grant, our distinguished leaders would be too fat to fit into their plush leather chairs, and probably too drunk to even find the Capitol. With numbers that large, however, the game has grown beyond the simple food and drink social gatherings. Sheer competition requires that a bigger price than that be paid for favorable votes. And you can bet your next paycheck that the good ol' boys like it that way!

Even as inherently weak as this lobbying regulation law is, the wise old birds who wrote it provided some really neat loopholes. Listen to this portion of the Act, which helps the hunters to take an unlimited bag from the gang:

> The provisions of this section (reporting of expenditures) shall not apply . . . to any public official acting in his official capacity . . . or any individual who owns,

> publishes, or is employed by any [such] newspaper or periodical . . . which publishes news items, editorials or other comments or paid advertisements . . .

In that short stretch in the Lobbying Regulation Act, paraphrased for clarity, a gaping loophole is created for many who actively lobby for specific legislation or contracts. Through liberal interpretation by those who benefit most from the millions of lobbying dollars, literally thousands are exempted from any regulation of their lobbying efforts.

This simple loophole allows all members of the Republican and Democrat national and state committees, as "public officials" to lobby Congress at will without regulation. This friendly provision, plus the broad blanket exemption granted the news media, has left the door wide open for "no-holds barred" secret lobbying. To see just how the party insiders take advantage of the lush earning opportunity presented by this loophole we'll take a look at the Republican Party's own "Charlie Keating," William Taylor, National GOP Committeeman from Florida.

Chapter 11
Party of Opportunity

With the headlines and prime time concentrating on big name scandals relating to government, there is a tendency to overlook even worse corruption with less national entertainment value. Charlie Keating and his five senatorial playmates are well exposed, and the reams of print and hours of TV bring forth a satisfying level of indignation from all. We had weeks of exciting prime time on departed Congressman Jim Wright and Tony Coelho with much applause for, and grateful bowing from, those who drove the two former national leaders out. All of this does marvelous things for circulation and TV poll ratings.

Since most of these stories are treated more for their entertainment value than for the more sobering effect on our very system of government, we learn more than we ever really wanted to know about such media stars as failed presidential candidate and former senator Gary Hart. What most of us don't see are the far more numerous and shocking stories concerning scandal and corruption on the part of the lesser-known figures. One of these, small in the eyes of the media but large in the warping of our system, is William Taylor, Republican Party official, convicted briber, and acknowledged influence peddler.

The William Taylors in our political system are so numerous, although generally unnoticed, that they present a problem in many ways more dangerous to our whole governing system than all the Senators linked to Keating. For that reason we need to take some time on the Taylor story, even at the risk of turning him into a household word like "Charlie."

My first contact with William (Bill) Taylor came a number of years ago when he was a member of the Florida Republican State Committee, representing Duval County, home of rapidly developing Jacksonville. Bill, at the time, was an independent insurance adjuster, not doing very well in competition with the big insurance companies who did their own adjusting. Physically Taylor was the image of the storied traveling salesman. Inclined to pudginess, he was given to chomping on odorous cigars and telling off-color stories.

Like many in the politically active lower ranks of the party, Bill laid the groundwork for his future at the county committee level before getting elected to the state GOP. Also typical of most party activists, Taylor never evidenced any interest in seeking public office, although the ability and personality for public campaigning were certainly there. He chose, instead, the rough-and-tumble, often bloody, infighting so common in the maneuvering for power on the inside of our political parties. In view of later developments in the career of this ruthless political manipulator, I have no doubt Taylor knew from the very start the probability of substantial rewards inside the system as he set out to plow under anyone standing in his way.

Bill quite adroitly lined up votes from the majority of his State GOP Committee to get elected chairman of the party. Coming from north Florida himself, he played upon the natural rural/urban split within the party. Shamelessly he won over the small county members (who carry the majority vote in the Republican Party's highly biased system) by appealing to their own ingrown dislike of the urban (mostly "carpetbagger" northerners in their minds) population of heavily settled south Florida. In keeping with his campaign as one of the north Florida "rednecks," he took to wearing cowboy boots and a ten-gallon hat. In his western style getup he built a solid party base as he railed against the Miami "city slickers" trying to take over the party. Although effective, this was not an original approach with Taylor. Since Republican Party rules have always favored the rural areas in every state, many of the party's national leaders had long ago adopted that good ol' boy facade. Such GOP party leaders as Lyn Nofziger and Republican National Chairman Lee Atwater have long used the same act to vault themselves into power.

Bill Taylor came into the chairmanship of the Florida GOP while it was still generally staffed and run by unpaid, dedicated amateurs. Not letting any grass grow under his feet, while he still had an overwhelming majority vote on the committee, he quickly had his position turned into a paying job with generous expense allowances. Continuing to play the part of a country redneck at party meetings, behind the scenes he converted the state organization into a money maker for the insiders. At one open meeting, when a member of the committee had the temerity to question some budget expenditures, Taylor quickly used the power of his position by disbanding the audit committee and taking personal charge of all party funds.

No longer under pressure to earn his former meager living in the insurance business, Bill devoted himself assiduously to being a full time GOP chairman. Now he began to sport custom-tooled cowboy boots, hand-tailored western suits and imported cowboy hats. When asked by a committee member how he managed a new Mercedes-Benz automobile, he airily brushed the question aside by declaring it was "loaned" to him by a party benefactor.

During this period under Taylor, he moved the party into massive, computer-controlled mail fundraising, now so common to the whole party. The annual budgets of the state GOP moved into the multimillion dollar bracket, whereas before Taylor the annual cost of operation seldom reached $200,000! Not surprising, in view of the way it was handled by the inside cadre, a 2,000 percent increase in money flow didn't show a corresponding increase in the amounts actually spent on elections, supposedly a political party's primary mission. You get an idea about how personal income for the insiders was enhanced when you note the party's paid executive director and "volunteer" chief fundraiser owned controlling interests in the mailing and computer firms that received the well-paid contracts from the Taylor-run Republican committee. It's also noteworthy that during Taylor's reign Republican candidates for public office were made well aware of the importance of having their campaign mailing pieces processed by the insider-controlled mailing firm. One thing that could always be said about Bill Taylor, he was not very subtle, candidates knew where they had to spend the funds provided by the party through their fundraising on the candidate's behalf! Although as Chairman of the State Republican Committee, Taylor had an automatic seat on the GOP National Committee, local party duties were beginning to encroach upon the time he could devote to his own side income. The fringe benefits at the state level were substantial, but they couldn't hold a candle to the far greater opportunities available in Washington! To capitalize on the real money-making possibilities at the national level, Bill took up the craft of lobbying.

As a lobbyist, Taylor was one of those "public officials" exempted under the Lobbying Act, and he was free to spend unlimited amounts to gain favors for his employers without the bothersome necessity of making a public disclosure! To give himself more time in Washington to work this gold mine, Bill gave up his party chairmanship for the less time-consuming position of National Committeeman. To make sure the home fires continued to burn properly, he used his clout to maneuver Mrs. Jeannie Austin into his vacated seat as chairman.

You are probably wondering, at this point, of what use was membership on the National Republican Committee if he was going to function as a paid lobbyist anyway? I'm glad you asked. This is where the whole political system really turns sour, and almost completely without any notice from the public, or even for that matter, from the many thousands of dedicated party volunteers who think the sun rises and sets on their committees.

The national political parties are conduits for literally hundreds of millions of dollars constantly flowing into the system. With untold, and unknown even to sophisticated political activists, subcommittees set up to raise and dispense funds, the national parties wield an influence over public officeholders that make Keating's purchase of the willing five look like amateurism. Keep in mind that only a tiny fraction of this money ever gets onto any kind of public report. Able to pump a million dollars or more into a single race for the Senate or a governorship, and nearly comparable amounts into lesser contests, you can be sure our distinguished officeholders treat these committees with great respect.

Who gets to decide where all this clandestine money goes? I bet you're already ahead of me on that one, none other than to our hard working committee members like William Taylor! Since the political parties use the same antiquated seniority system as our Congress in handing out the important insider positions, you can see how a relatively long-term member like Taylor builds power. That rank in the inner sanctum was used to take a commanding position when the decisions had to be made as to which candidate got the money and how much. That's where Bill, and many more like him, attained his persuasive power over Washington officeholders.

When that inside ability to determine distribution of the millions in the party's secret coffers is combined with a lobbying position, the conflict of interest is beyond justification. Even the slowest thinkers in Congress and the top administrative positions soon learn how to subvert the best interests of good government to their opportunity for personal economic enhancement. As they do the things necessary to satisfy the insider lobbyist, the organizations retaining that lobbyist, seeing their wishes come true, are generous with their fees. It's hard to forget the astronomical "retainers" paid to the likes of former Texas Senator John Tower, and former Interior Secretary James Watt as they explained to Congressional Committees that those hundreds of thousands of dollars were paid to them to make a few "friendly" phone calls to government leaders.

Bill Taylor's start in the lobbying business came when he was retained by the city of Jacksonville to secure favorable Washington action on federal grants they sought for local projects. To the uninitiated, being a lobbyist for a city the size of Jacksonville doesn't look like any big deal, but they paid him over $80,000 annually over a number of years. That should give you an idea about the kind of money local governments are tapping Uncle Sam for.

The pickings for Taylor, with the persuasive influence of all that GOP party money behind him, grew rapidly. Sadly enough, like so many others in his shoes (er, cowboy boots), the sellout of our Congress and other top Washington officials became so blatant it seemed there would never be a limit on what could be made at influence peddling. The flamboyant committeeman became so arrogantly confident of his own power that he aroused the ire of a senator from his own state who had him banned from her office. Former U.S. Senator Paula Hawkins told me that Taylor constantly barged into her office, unannounced, demanding she exercise her influence on behalf of one of his benefactors. When he openly spoke of seeing that envelopes containing substantial amounts of cash would appear on her desk in response to favorable action, she exploded in anger and had him banned permanently from her Senate office.

When Senator Hawkins lost her bid for reelection in 1986, it was widely known within the Republican Party that National Committeeman Bill Taylor and his close associate State Chairman Austin had sat on their hands during the campaign.

Taylor's insatiable lust for money caught up with him in 1987 when he finally reached beyond the bounds of protection from the good ol' boy system. The cigar chomping Florida cowboy approached a New Jersey hotel developer, Gerald von Dohlen, promising to use his Washington power to get a $4.4 million dollar grant approved for Jacksonville, under which von Dohlen would receive a contract to build a luxury hotel and convention center for the city. Working both sides of the fence, Taylor was already receiving $84,000 per year from Jacksonville to get the same grant through, and then he advised von Dohlen he only needed to slip $25,000 cash to the GOP official to have a deal!

The contractor, not taking too kindly to Taylor's double-dipping bribe request, went directly to the local State's Attorney to report the illegal solicitation. The local law enforcement office fitted him with a hidden microphone and tape recorder and had him set up another meeting with Taylor. At that meeting, von Dohlen passed $5,000 in cash to Taylor as a down payment on his $25,000 bribe! Nailed with the damning recording, GOP leader Bill Taylor had no defense as he was indicted and set for trial.

William Taylor, facing the inevitable, entered a plea of "no contest." The friendly local prosecutor arranged the plea bargain on the flimsy excuse that Taylor, at 65, was too old to have to go to jail! The Court accepted the plea and after paying a $5,000 fine Taylor was turned loose to ply his influence peddling routes as usual.

The city of Jacksonville, not as solicitous of Taylor's age as the court, canceled his $84,000 per year contract and banned him from any further lobbying in the city. In view of events to be revealed later, this turned out to be as light a slap on the wrist as the one administered by the Judge.

At this point it appeared to be a straightforward case of a petty official getting caught in the cookie jar, although $25,000 bribes and $84,000 would look like pretty significant cookies to most people. Common decency would dictate that this should have been the end of Bill Taylor, at least as far as the political system was concerned. The sickening part of the affair is that it not only wasn't the end, it didn't even cause him or his political party to show even token signs of remorse or apology to their supporters. Taylor's public reaction to the affair was just some more of his quick quips, and his party leaders followed suit.

Mrs. Jeannie Austin, Co-Chairman of the Republican National Committee wasted no time getting to the press to defend and excuse Taylor's actions. Speaking to members of the fourth estate she stoutly maintained that Taylor's conviction and subsequent reactions from the city of Jacksonville would not affect his standing in the Republican Party! Emphasizing her, and the Party's official position she stated, "As I understand it, it was like a small conflict-of-interest thing and I don't see it affecting anything."

Fired from an $84,000 lobby deal and banned from future city work, nailed for a $25,000 bribe—just a small "conflict-of-interest thing"—what a landmark statement of political ethics! It is interesting to note that same attitude was current among our top government leaders as they brushed off Jim Wright's sordid behavior as just a "book deal thing" and former Congressman Tony Coelho's activities as just a "junk bond thing"! Given the immoral mind-set of our policymakers we can well expect Charlie Keating and his slippery five to eventually be brushed aside as just a "Savings and Loan thing"!

Little details like losing $84,000 per year and being permanently banned from lobbying in his home city apparently didn't phase the former insurance man, as subsequent events reveal. True to GOP leader Austin's statement, the local disgrace and court conviction seemed to have no effect on Taylor's ability to swing the inside power of his political party for his own personal gain.

Bill Taylor became something of a national figure the year after his bribery conviction as the huge financial scandal in the U.S. Department of Housing and Urban Development hit the prime time news. Called as a witness before the House Government Operations Committee, charged with influence peddling, the portly, cigar chomping Republican leader showed the prior scandals had done little to deflate his arrogance. With the TV cameras whirring, he proudly maintained that he had made over $800,000 using his influence over federal officials on behalf of developers from Georgia to Texas. He proudly testified that he saw nothing wrong with making money from politics, acknowledging using the Republican National Committee and Party power in Washington to "bring home the bacon" for his generous benefactors. Admitting he called the White House when necessary to get further contacts to aid his well-paying friends, he brushed it all off with the statement, "This is Washington!"

And that, unfortunately, is Washington! Millions of dollars are routinely being passed to line the pockets of insiders selling out our governing process as they do their "Washington thing"!

With the Taylor court conviction and the Congressional disgrace of Representatives Jim Wright and Tony Coelho, I tried to contact the leadership of both national political parties for comments. Repeated phone calls asking for statements concerning the official party positions on ethical standards got me no further than the party's press officers. In both parties their response was uniform, they could not speak for their organizations' policy positions. I was repeatedly promised return phone calls from higher authority, and I'm still waiting!

The Republican Party of Florida, since Taylor's bribery conviction and his involvement in the reeking HUD scandals, has tried to remove him from his position as the state's representative on their National Committee, but with little success. Although the attempt was motivated more by the fact that Taylor has not been a loyal supporter of GOP Governor Bob Martinez, rather than by any strong ethical indignation, their efforts have failed as the National Republican Committee insiders rally round to protect one of their own.

Along with the Keating Five Scandals, the Bill Taylor affairs will probably fade away as the news media moves ever onward to new sensations. We will, of course, continue to read about, and see in living color, pious announcements from Washington leaders concerning their progress on tightening ethical standards in Government. Many billions of tax dollars will be earmarked to save failing savings and loans, and shoring up corrupt government housing projects. These billions will be spent with long appropriate speeches from concerned leaders showing their deep concern for us average-type citizens. Don't, however, hold your breath expecting the same swift movement to put the senators, congressman and party officials out of their lucrative side businesses draining those same dollars.

Chapter 12

Honoraria without Honor

Lest we get the impression that all corruption of our governing system comes from evil outsiders applying unbearable pressure on our leaders, we must look at the ingenious enterprise of our elected elite in improving their personal financial standing, through what are called "honoraria." Like so many frequently used twists in the English language employed by Washington insiders, it is near impossible to trace the source of the term. One thing you can be assured of though, with this and other terms in common usage on the shores of the Potomac, the label seldom gives a hint of the true content.

Like the classic governmentese of "revenue enhancement" to disguise a tax increase, "honoraria" is used to cover a universal Washington practice as far from "honor" as Mars is from Venus.

Like many subjects our leaders would prefer we not become too learned on, it's hard to pinpoint just when the practice of paying cash "honoraria" to elected and high appointed government officials for personal appearances began. We do know that early in the development of our system, members of the House of Representatives and the Senate were happy to devote much of their time to appearing before groups of constituents, at no charge, to expound upon those things they were doing or hoped to do in Congress. Somewhere along the line it was discovered that offering a cash payment to the senator or congressman not only increased their availability for such personal appearances, but for some obvious reasons it also increased the frequency of favorable actions by these policy and law makers.

The Washington penchant for obscuring the meaning within our language caused another revision, as "constituent" acquired a new definition. Once a term commonly understood to mean someone from the elected official's home territory, whose vote helped place that leader in office, "constituent" has been broadened to mean any individual or group who can provide a positive supplement to the politician's income or standard of living. This definition has reached its broadest sweep in the case of the Keating Five who have all dutifully excused their actions as ordinary constituent service!

When distinguished leaders, such as U.S. House Majority Whip, Representative William Gray of Pennsylvania, manage to make six trips to Florida (in the cold of winter, naturally) during one year, with all expenses paid by the AMA (American Medical Association), this, of course, is referred to as normal constituent service. You realize, naturally, that the constituent doctors in attendance at these meetings do not expect to hear their political guests tell them any bad news about the fees they draw from the federal Medicare programs. To make sure these distinguished paid guests understand the problems of their specialized constituents, much consulting time is scheduled on the pleasant golf courses common to these meeting places. These constituents frequently show their deep understanding of the great strain our governing leaders are under when they generously provide their guests with new sets of golf clubs for more complete relaxation on these outings! We should all feel a deep sense of pride that these struggling doctors and hard-pressed legislators are able to break away from their normal drudgery for these pleasant exchanges of ideas. I'm sure the shivering voting constituents back in Pennsylvania also get a warm feeling knowing their representative is able to escape his grueling schedule in Washington so frequently.

Realizing that all-expense family vacations, or even free golf clubs, are really not enough to express their appreciation of the wonderful job being done in Washington, concerned constituent groups, such as the AMA, take that extra step so necessary for the happiness of our government leaders. A $2,000 or more cash gift is made to the honored visitor, so that the trip should not be merely a "breakeven" vacation. Rather than label these cash windfalls for what they really are (we'll leave a blank here so you can fill in your own definition) our distinguished leaders refer to the pocketed cash as "honoraria."

Starting as a relatively modest gift to visiting public officeholders who provided after-dinner speeches at conventions, influence buyers at all levels soon learned that "honoraria" paid off many times the dollar investment in favorable decisions from the government leaders honored. No longer do congressmen or senators need to be eloquent or amusing speakers to get on the large payoff lists. The key factor in all the invitations is: How important is the guest's vote or influence on other votes in their legislative body? Even the most tongue-tied boobs of Washington find themselves with more invitations than they can handle to "come pick up your check"! The buyers, competing in a seller's market, finding there was not enough time or locations to schedule major dinner meetings, now pay the willing influence peddlers out of Washington for token appearances at small lunches and breakfasts. Apparently not wanting to go to all the trouble of traveling to numerous scattered meetings to pick up his checks, a few years ago Senator Lloyd Bentsen (TX) decided to lump the payoffs into a more easily manageable package. His plan was to invite all the buyers to come to one common breakfast with him, and to bring their checkbooks along.

Some years ago, in a small concession to public indignation at the way they collected truly obscene amounts from the special interest buyers, Congress instituted some small measures to limit total honoraria. These limits, although still allowing our leaders to pocket tens of thousands of dollars in payoffs every year, are still more noted for their violation than honest compliance. Always showing a remarkable ability to innovate methods of enhancing their personal wealth, seldom seen in their actions for the public on the floors on Congress, the Washington elite lost little time in getting around their own mandated limitations.

Sometimes the dodges used to exceed the honoraria limits are simple. Now when the pleasure-seeking congressmen and senators come in from their exhausting afternoons on the golf course or fishing yachts to render their sleep-provoking speeches, they are paid "travel" expenses in lieu of honoraria. Some years ago I recall an eastern senator after a singularly unsuccessful speech before a local Republican committee, asking the party chairman to mark his $5,000 check as "expense reimbursement," rather than as an honorarium as originally agreed upon. He obviously had reached his "honoraria" limit and had a bookkeeping problem! The chairman indignantly refused, and forwarded the check marked as a fee, I never heard whether this presented any reporting problem for the senator! Overall, the "travel" expenses being collected by our designated leaders would send the entire Congress around the world several times over.

In all fairness, however, most of our elected lawmakers show a much better flair for innovation than the simplistic "expense thing." Former House Majority Leader Jim Wright of Texas, for example, went the publishing route. Wright, using his substantial Congressional staff, had a collection of his singularly unnotable speeches compiled into book form.

Turning to a friendly printer (who, only incidentally received other, more lucrative printing contracts through the powerful Congressman) he had the book printed under a deal guaranteeing him 55 percent royalties! That alone was enough to draw raised eyebrows, since few legitimate writers can wrangle more than 10 percent royalties from their efforts. Wright's angle included a simple plan to insure heavy sales, hence personal royalties, of the non-bestseller. Influence buyers were given the opportunity to purchase carloads of his book in lieu of honoraria in excess of his annual limitation. The beauty of this truly clever deal can best be appreciated when you realize the Texas wheeler-dealer had probably already collected honoraria for most of the dull speeches when originally delivered! That is known as having your cake and eating it too.

Less imaginative was the dodge used by former Congressman Jack Kemp of New York, when he found himself about to exceed the honoraria limitations during his last year in Congress. This insider, picked by President George Bush to head the scandal-ridden Department of Housing and Urban Development (HUD), simply instructed his benefactors to postdate their checks so he could pick up the illegally excess income in the following year. Secretary Kemp was able to pocket an extra $60,000 above the legal honoraria limit through this simple expedient. The former professional football quarterback displayed his open-field running ability when he casually brushed off this illegal bonanza by claiming it was simply a "misinterpretation" of the law! This nifty swivel hipping is noteworthy in that Congressman Kemp was there, and a supporter, when Congress instituted the legal limits on honoraria! Unfortunately, his attitude is not at all atypical of the general contempt our elected leaders have for the intelligence of those who put them in office.

Former Congressman Tony Coelho (CA) resigned from office when his method of avoiding the reporting limits surfaced. Strangely enough, Coelho's personal enrichment plan is probably the most used of all the deals our leaders make to increase their personal wealth. He was given the opportunity to buy a quantity of bonds at a favorable price through insiders seeking to buy influence from him, which he soon sold at substantial profits. This one is frequent, as many insiders are given the opportunity to invest in real estate and business deals on the side that become astoundingly profitable after a favorable act or government purchase comes about through help from the elected leader. This is undoubtedly the most difficult of all the influence peddling schemes to detect. If you want to do some side research on the subject, take a look at the number of congressman who, during their relatively short time in Congress, rise from modest financial status to multimillionaire rating. Even they will admit they could not have done it on their modest government salary.

Even though the general news media occasionally raise questions concerning the greening of Congress through honoraria and related payoffs, by and large the big guns in the business wink at the process. As it turns out, there are good and ample reasons for the news moguls' kindly treatment of these open payoffs: they're working the same lucrative gold mines themselves. Major TV talking heads, many news editors, and most syndicated print columnists make many personal appearances before select groups. Most of these generous organizations are the same pressure groups that buy the undying friendship of our Washington elite through generous honoraria. I have yet to find one of these insider members of the news media who do not ask for and receive substantial fees plus expenses for their personal appearances. Although seldom heard in public or reported in the media, this common practice of public opinion molders is being more and more criticized within their own closed fraternity.

It is well accepted, and seldom questioned, that the votes of members of Congress are seriously affected by the substantial gifts of cash funneled their way by those promoting interests not necessarily in the public interest. But what about the media stars of TV and print news and commentary? It doesn't take a special poll to learn that these national opinion molders are expressing specific viewpoints and policies of their own or their employers. It's also a given that they can reach an audience far larger than that touched by all but a few members of Congress. But tools of the big buck operators buying our government? How can that be?

Let's use the hypothetical case of nationally syndicated columnist Archibald Smoothwriter, whose sterling prose appears weekly in 150 newspapers serving the major readership markets of the country. Archie, through his hardworking agent, is made available to the same rubber chicken circuit traveled by your very own senator. The difference with Archie, however, is that he is so well known, instead of the paltry $2,000 to $5,000 honoraria offered your senator, he demands and gets $10,000 to $20,000 or more!

When the Amalgamated Widget Association of America holds its annual convention in fun-filled Las Vegas, Smoothwriter is invited to be their featured speaker (no quarrel over his substantial fee and expenses). Archie does his usual routine, titillating the widget gang with inside anecdotes casually proving he regularly rubs shoulders with the power elite in Washington. It's just coincidence, of course, that at this convention the widgeteers make sure their guest understands their concern about the impact cheap widgets from Lower Slobbovia are making on their domestic market. The message is duly noted by our columnist as he accepts his fat appearance check.

In due course Archibald Smoothwriter's nationally distributed columns are deploring the Slobbovian widgets and the adverse effects these lower-cost products are having on the old established American widget industry. In his attention-getting style he calls for government action to return America (flags waving, bugles blaring) to its former preeminence in widgets! On one of the Sunday morning TV talk shows, where Archie appears regularly, he joins in the panel's interview of Senator Available, Chairman of the powerful Senate Widget Committee. The syndicated columnist, with his famous sneer and raised eyebrows, directs pointed and hard hitting questions at the distinguished senator concerning the "Widget Crisis." The senator, in his well-known reasoned and placating tones, staring wide-eyed and guilelessly into the camera, assures the popular columnists and the national TV audience that he will leave no stone unturned to get a bill through Congress blocking off those job-stealing Lower Slobbovians! Is there a conflict of interest here? Read on.

Behind the scenes, concern by some media members over their own "honoraria thing" is being systematically and ruthlessly squelched as the fourth estate rallies round to protect their insider perks, just as the good ol' boys in Congress do. Not long ago, reporters accorded credentials to work in the hallowed halls of Congress were fighting among themselves over whether to tighten the virtually nonexistent rules on identifying outside sources of income. During this inside-the-family media battle, three outspoken reporters pressing for honest reporting of conflicting outside income were summarily kicked off the organization's executive committee! The majority of this select group wanted no part in disclosing their conflict of interest outside income!

Former Congressman Tony Coelho (CA), stung by the news media's double standard in protecting themselves while criticizing public officials for conflicts, exploded in an interview, "While the latter-day Lord Actons wrote that honoraria corrupt Congress, and paid travel corrupts absolutely, they voted to continue collecting speech fees and enjoying travel to plush resorts—without disclosure—as if their objectivity could never be questioned."

The Congressman concluded, "Under their system, you can't kill the messenger (the media), but it's okay to bribe him in secret!"

This "holier than thou" attitude on the part of the media was best expressed on a recent "Inside Washington" network TV panel discussion. The moderator asked his regular panel member, nationally syndicated columnist James Kilpatrick, the question, "Should journalists reveal the fees they get for giving speeches?"

Kilpatrick's response was immediate, and delivered with obvious anger, "No! It's nobody's business but mine!"

The rest of the discussion panel, openly embarrassed by Kilpatrick's crusty response, feebly tried to gloss over the subject. Their party line was that any positions they took were merely personal opinions and couldn't possibly influence anyone! Nice going, guys and gals, there lies a ready made excuse for all those national leaders making impassioned speeches on the floors of Congress. They're only personal opinions and don't affect anyone.

The defensive attitude of the media stars was expressed again, albeit with more aplomb, when TV panel host David Brinkley asked a similar question of his cohorts Sam Donaldson and George Will. The pointed question from their folksy leaders died aborning as his two megastars killed the subject indicating they felt it unworthy of discussion.

As bad as the acknowledged honoraria are, the constant light of publicity on that phase of the sale of our government tends to cover up the criminal disgrace of many even more serious practices. Earlier, in the Keating saga, we touched upon the elaborate complex owned and run by prime government contractor, Rockwell International Corporation. Their luxurious complex in the Bahamas, only one of a number of hideaway centers they operated, existed almost exclusively for the purpose of lavishing tender loving care on willing government officials and their families. Run unemotionally as business operations, these divisions were required to pay off in benefits to the corporation every bit as much as any of their actual production factories. These resort-type complexes were tightly managed with highly trained professional staffs primed to see that all desires of their guests were fulfilled. The corporate scheduling office for these well hidden assets was as professional as any major travel agency, always seeing that the proper people were scheduled in with the least disturbance and publicity possible. Year round amenities, such as golf, swimming, deep-sea fishing, and hunting (at their more northernmost operation), were supplemented by the very finest in wining and dining, matching any five-star commercial operation!

Operations, such as Rockwell's, which have no productive function other than wooing buyers of the company's product or services are not unique just to that giant government contractor. Although relatively few actually run their own complete resort-type operations, it is more common for those doing business with our Washington elite to own condominiums and homes at exotic resorts for the same purposes.

Since our neophyte political officeholders are trained early in the process to look for the good life from those seeking favors from their governing position, it is not unusual to find "mini-Rockwell" facilities at the very lowest level of the political system. In one area of south Florida, William Knight, a local land developer, provides similar pleasant additions to the lifestyles of those he does business with. Just as with the big swingers working the Washington territory, Knight's generously provided diversions seem to be mostly for those hard-pressed public officials who hold positions where their authority can provide helpful action on his petitions for zoning and building favors.

Knight's medium for providing much-needed R and R to his guests is a completely equipped and staffed deep-sea fishing yacht. Every year the Knight Enterprises office mails out engraved invitations (mostly to mayors, city councilmen, and county commissioners) offering the honored ones the opportunity to sign up for one- or two-week trips to wondrous destinations such as the Virgin Islands for blue marlin fishing or the Bahamas for bluefin tuna fun under the sun. To make sure his elite know exactly what they are getting, the invitations include a chatty newsletter detailing all the good times the prior year's guests had on their trips!

These pleasant diversions provided regularly to our government decision makers (and the elite news media leaders as well) seldom appear on any official reports. Although there is a fair amount of public discussion and moralizing over the practice of accepting cash honoraria for appearances at nongovernmental affairs, there is a uniform silence over the even greater value of the expensive vacations and "meetings" provided by the influence buyers. Even though Congress and most state officeholders are required to report gifts exceeding token amounts, these pleasurable, out of the way, outings seldom appear on the official reports. Similarly, corporate aircraft and limousines provided for the comfortable transport of favored officeholders seem to miss the reports.

If we really are going to concern ourselves with honoraria we'd better understand that it encompasses far more than the check or envelope of cash following another rubber chicken speech.

Chapter 13

Soft (?) Money

While the volumes of cash and the size of expensive perks being showered on our greedy politicians is certainly not chicken feed by any reckoning, the so-called "soft" money flowing through political channels is beyond normal understanding. Although honoraria, expense allowances, and luxury vacations run into tens of thousands of dollars and constitute a serious threat to our constitutional system, the soft money pay-off flow more often runs into hundreds of thousands and even millions of dollars!

Origin of the term "soft" money is difficult to trace. Relying on the *American Heritage Dictionary*, we see a number of definitions for "soft." Its usage in the current text may come from the old term of "soft" currency, meaning paper money as opposed to gold or silver ("hard" currency). Since it would be impossible to find any of our political leaders opposed to accepting paper currency, no matter how proffered, this definition would appear redundant. Another definition for "soft" is "not loud, or strident: low toned." This one does come close, since the media-coined term "soft" money applies to huge doses of cash changing hands quietly without benefit of public scrutiny. Still, "soft" does not seem to fit the reality of the practice. Taking advantage of literary license, let's settle on a term that better describes the product and its function—hidden money. Since it makes no public appearance or accounting, and much effort is expended by both the giver and the taker to keep it hidden, let's run with it! You will have to use your own best judgment in expanding upon this definition by deciding whether it is clean or dirty as it moves through the inner political tunnels, although you would not be faulted for questioning why clean money needs to be hidden from public view.

As pointed out earlier, when the clever gaggle of political minds in Congress gathered in close harmony to orchestrate our election and campaign finance laws, they made sure there was plenty of room for the silent chorus. As weak as the basic rules under which the Federal Election Commission operates are, there have been glaring loopholes provided so the abuses we're examining can run unchecked. Without getting into minute detail on the many pages of regulations, it is sufficient to note that no restrictions apply to the amount of money raised or spent if you claim it is not for the "direct" purpose of electing an individual or group of candidates. Since no rules apply to raising or expending money outside this narrowly interpreted provision, such funds do not come under any reporting or accounting regulation. This well-calculated opening became the birthplace of "soft," or as we have designated it, "hidden" money.

Approaching major election years, the air fills with one of the favorite themes of ambitious politicians. Although the words vary slightly from performance to performance, the major melody is consistent. The arias, heavy with soothing background music dominated by violins and other muted instruments spread the "Testing the Waters" or "Weighing the Options" theme so popular in the cultural world of politics. These performances usually precede announcements of "independent" study committees or more lofty research foundations to study major policy positions in line with the mood of the electorate. These learned studies, professed to be nonpartisan in nature, outline the kind of performance the voting public expects from their elected representative in a specific office. Even though Senator (or would-be Senator) Blowhard formed the research group and staffed it with friends or relatives, the operators are very careful to explain to all who will listen, they are nonpartisan and not promoting Uncle

Blowhard. Having thus met the requirements under our fuzzy laws, they are free to raise and expend unlimited amounts of money without public accounting. While not bluntly asking for the support of Blowhard, they are free to impress upon the influence buyers who constitute their best source of funds, that their altruistic goals are dear to the heart of Gideon Blowhard who is widely reported to be ready to run for the U.S. Senate!

There are far too many of these "nonpartisan," mostly secret, organizations to enumerate; however, a few have recently drawn more publicity than their sponsors ever wanted to see. Senator Alan Cranston, representing California and Charlie Keating, has a thriving organization of this genre. With the highly impressive name of "Center for Participation in Democracy," Senator Cranston's private foundation, whose paid director just happens to be his son, has been singularly successful in raising and spending large sums of money. This "public service" Cranston organization has the stated purpose of persuading laggard citizens to register to vote. It would be a shockingly misinformed donor who did not understand the pleasure and gratitude his donation to this high-minded group would give to the senator, let alone his son!

Without even getting into the marvelous training grounds these "independent" organizations provide for the eventual campaign workers or staff of the organizer, or the everlasting gratitude and support they buy for the donors, there is another important benefit not usually available to the big money movers in the political system. Since trusts or foundations like Cranston's are supposedly "public service" in nature, they have been declared tax-exempt by the U.S. Internal Revenue Service. This means that those influence buyers who follow these routes to the heart of their favorite government representative not only gain favor from the representative in question, they can list their purchase as a tax deduction item on their annual IRS returns. You talk about having your cake and being able to eat it too! The heavy cash flow in these scams, both coming and going, slips through without any sharing by IRS. Try that one on your weekly paycheck if you can!

But, let us not approach this from a purely selfish viewpoint. We should all have a warm feeling knowing that good old Charlie Keating was able to support this worthy cause of one of his favorite Senators without that nasty old IRS taking a bite out of his $1 million. Unfortunately, no matter how sympathetic we are, it seems that nosy federal agencies such as the FBI, and even, belatedly, the IRS, are beginning to scrutinize Senator Cranston's benevolent organization. There seems to be some question about how nonpartisan this nonprofit group has been. Surprisingly, after all these years they seem to be taking note of the fact that the Cranston family group has been placing undue emphasis on registering Democrat voters. We can assume this is just another one of those embarrassing coincidences so common to our governing elite, since the good senator also happens to be a Democrat. With all due respect, let us give credit where credit is deserved: This whole matter would not have surfaced without the sordid story of Charlie Keating, close personal friend and benefactor to Senator Alan Cranston.

In continued fairness, and not to confine all our bashing to Senator Cranston, we must point out that the private plaything of Senator John Glenn of Ohio also received a substantial helping hand from good old Charlie. The generous Keating, not one to play favorites, managed to drop off $200,000 to the astronaut senator's group in passing. It isn't only Charlie's Angels who have special organizations waiting with open doors to receive the big checks that grease our political wheels, they are a substantial industry within our system. The political news media, especially the elite Washington corps, are well aware of these hidden money dodges run by government policy makers. There seems to be an unspoken agreement to keep these side functions out of the public eye as far as possible. Only when something as attention getting as the Keating affair comes along do they deign to wax eloquent over the abusive nature of this form of political cash flow. Like ever-circling vultures, our guardians of the fourth estate don't pounce until the victim is already near death and unable to strike back.

As big as these private hidden money operations are, they pale into insignificance when we open the door on the murky closets of our two major political parties. It is within these influence wielding political think tanks that hiding the corrupting dollars has been developed into a high art form. A great deal is heard about the fund-raising prowess, or lack thereof, of the Republican and Democrat National Committees. As they regularly file their reports with the Federal Elections Commission, the media does much "oh"ing and "ah"ing over the "war chests" accumulated by the two all-powerful insider organizations. And even though the public reports deal in many millions of dollars, they are literally only petty cash when compared to the hundreds of millions in hidden funds.

Federal election laws require public reporting of only those funds actually earmarked or used for election campaigns for federal office. Money not used directly in federal elections, or used for state and local campaigns, does not have to be accounted for. With fifty state committees and uncounted local committees, the two major political parties have an unlimited range of outlets for their funds. Not unlike the confusing maze created by launderers of illegal drug money, it is impossible to trace the dollars jumping from one committee resting spot to another. The criminally lax and almost nonexistent state and local regulations pertaining to political funds is very helpful to insiders wishing to hide "who gave it" and "who got it." If you don't know where it came from or where it went, you cannot pinpoint exactly what it bought. Also helpful in concealing the bidding operation on our government has been the interpretation of "direct" election expenses. Not unexpectedly in today's swinging political financing, the insiders have found more "indirect" expenses to keep off the record than those that need be reported.

The plethora of committees, including dozens of direct subcommittees of the two national parties, provide more than enough avenues for creative financing of our elected leaders. By far the most popular route for the hidden money is the fiction of indirect campaign expenditures. If you expend funds to tell the public to vote for Windbag for senator, you must file public reports on the dollars collected and spent. If, on the other hand, you tell the public to vote for the political party's candidates (even though Windbag is their only candidate) you can raise and spend the money in complete secrecy! This handy loophole in the Election Code has turned our national political committees into quasi-educational institutions. Most of the millions they disburse in secret are labeled for "voter education," "get out the vote," or "voter registration" drives. That our political leaders can run these shams with a straight face is probably the best illustration we could cite for the low level our system has reached!

During the 1988 presidential campaign, Robert Mosbacher, Sr., close personal friend of soon-to-be-President George Bush and long-time Republican inside powerhouse, served as candidate Bush's finance chairman. More importantly for the continuing power of the GOP insiders, he also served as chairman of the off-the-record hidden money generator, known inside the party as "Team 100." Membership on this "team" was open to all, the only requirement being that each potential member first had to give at least $100,000 to Mr. Mosbacher's hidden fund. That Mosbacher was singularly successful as captain of this team is attested by insider reports that this hidden fund exceeded $30 million by election time. This "educational" fund was expended to convince voters to vote for the Republican candidate (presumably without mentioning that Mr. Bush was that candidate)!

The Mosbacher-generated slush fund for the GOP insiders was only unusual in that some of those connected with it talked too much and suddenly it was no longer a well-kept secret. When Mosbacher was due to appear before the Senate for confirmation as President Bush's Secretary of Commerce, a political pressure group threatened to expose the "Team 100" membership and Mosbacher's inside fundraising activities. The GOP, breaking precedent, while attempting to downplay the public flap, issued a list of the "Team 100." Although attracting a flurry of clucking and tish-tishing by media pundits, the affair quietly faded out of the news as the new Administration moved on with other appointments. Ironically, the Mosbacher fund was only one of at least eight similar hidden funds within the Republican Party, and the others did not see the light of day.

In fairness, we must hasten to point out that the Republican Party does not stand alone as creative innovators with these hidden funds. In an obvious attempt to gain publicity and let the big buyers know they could find a home in the other party, the Democrats leaked the fact that Joan Kroc, heiress to the McDonald hamburger fortune, had given them $1 million for their insider activities.

The high bidders who write the weighty checks to these secret funds are generally praised by the political party insiders as public-spirited philanthropists who just want to anonymously support "good government." It might be cynical to point out here that their philosophy might lean more to the theory that the best government is the one I own. The total exposure of the makeup of the Mosbacher contributors gave the lie to such pious praise and created some real embarrassment for the GOP elite and President Bush. The president, after all, is himself a long-time Republican insider and once even served as National Committee Chairman. The red faces were created as questions were not only asked about Mosbacher's apparent rewarding appointment to the President's cabinet, but top donors on "Team 100" ended up with choice ambassador positions and other top administration appointments.

Any questions as to why the individuals on this exposed hidden fund team were so generous were quickly dispelled as the new administration began to form. At one point Mosbacher petulantly complained to the press that the White House staff was not rewarding enough of these big buyers with choice inside jobs. This, despite the fact that at the time of his complaint at least a dozen of the $100,000-plus bidders had already been tapped for top White House jobs. On top of that there was an additional "priority" list of over fifty major bidders who wanted jobs for themselves or their relatives.

The spoils system has long been a part of the United States political scene. It is expected that winning officeholders will favor friends and supporters with whatever jobs come under their jurisdictions. The practice in this modern age has grown beyond the realm of just rewards, however, to where top jobs and policy-making positions are openly up for sale to the highest bidder. This open market policy is best illustrated by the fact that many big donors to the GOP hidden funds also quietly gave substantial sums to the Democrats. When you're buying influence and position this practice is considered merely payment of an insurance premium!

Ideally, of course, we should be picking people to run our government who are qualified by experience, education, or intellect to make the important decisions that arise every day. Similarly we should expect our elected officials to make their important decisions based upon personal integrity rather than upon who paid the most. Pragmatically, we must accept that the best of all worlds is not within our reach, but that is not to imply we should meekly endure the worst.

Do we want a presidency run by key players who made the team solely through being the highest bidder with deposits into hidden funds? Do we want a Congress that makes decisions based upon who deposited the most into their private slush funds?

If we don't want our government on the trading block, what can be done about it? Will the inmates do anything to clean up their asylum?

Stay tuned!

Chapter 14
Will the Sellers Reform?

Nope!

Oops! The editor says I can't just drop it there!

He says he cannot understand how I can stand there (or sit at my word processor) with my bald face hanging out and say our esteemed leaders in Washington and the political parties are not going to clean up their act. He knows, from the news reports, just as you do, that our insider DL's (that's "Distinguished Leader" for those who like to use full titles) have been elbowing each other out of the camera's focus trying to express the most shock over the blatant financial abuses in the system coming to light every day. As you watch, they certainly all seem sincere, at least as sincere as they appeared when asking for your vote and, being well-trained passive citizens, we all want to believe their words. If you, and our editor, will bear with an indignant author for a few more pages let's question that sincerity.

After enough static from consumer interest groups and the folks back home, our congressional leaders finally attacked the subject of honoraria. Of course attack is probably too strong a term to apply to the wet-noodle lashing our astute insiders did to this popular form of payoff. Pulling out all the emotional stops bemoaning their severe financial sacrifice in the service of their country, the Washington gang managed to convince each other that honoraria only existed to help them pay the rent and clothe their shivering offspring. Following this line of logic, at least in Washington thinking, we, the public, were advised they would magnanimously give up their lucrative honoraria undercover income in return for a substantial pay increase. Seeing that their studied judgement was good on this, as in all things, they voted themselves a substantial pay increase so their struggling families would suffer no setback in their accustomed standard of living.

This "reform" somehow sounds little different than the bank president being forced to give a crooked teller a nice pay increase in order to stop him from stealing money from the bank customers' accounts! I see little difference here. The honoraria happily pocketed by our Washington insiders eventually becomes an expense item charged to some government contract or subsidy. And it's the taxpayers (us) who eventually pay those extra costs. We have raised our Congressmen's pay to stop their stealing from us. How much of this kind of "reform" can we stand?

Even with that much-praised "reform," our clever leaders didn't really close the door very tight. Rather than ban honoraria entirely, or, heaven forbid, declare it illegal, they opted for a protracted phase-out of this single source of side income. Carefully avoided in all these new rules of action on their part was closing the door on the happy practice of accepting large travel reimbursements for their many private appearances. Presumably all our senators and representatives will now instruct their benefactors to make the checks out to "travel." Our previously mentioned eastern senator who asked that his $5,000 stipend be marked "Travel—Washington to Florida" was just ahead of his time!

Of course, honoraria, now having been deemed officially dishonorable, is only a minor wart on a frog's back. The big money comes in other packaging, and those accustomed to providing the now unacceptable can still get the same amount into the hands of a willing seller in government by wrapping it differently!

Coming under prolonged frontal attack by political insiders, as well as the pious media, are "Political Action Committees." PACs are funds formed by pressure groups, unions, businesses, and even insider politicians, to funnel money to favorable officeholders, ostensibly to aid their election campaigns. Since PACs must file reports with the Federal Elections Commission, they are highly visible and make easy targets for news writers or TV commentators, too lazy, or not sharp enough to find all the other sources of money flowing into the system. It's not difficult, when trying to fill a dull period in a newscast or front page, to find an expert in the political system ready to launch into a lengthy diatribe on the evils of PACs. Whenever a microphone or reporter's pencil appears, your favorite Washington leader will oblige with an appropriate outrage against what PACs have done to our great American system, and then lean back for the mandatory applause from the grateful citizenry.

Beating up on PACs is like stomping cockroaches, you don't have to worry about anyone rising to their defense. When your own favorite senator or congressman proudly tells you of his part in this major "reform" you might pose some small rebuttal question, such as, "If PACs are such a prime source of evil in the buying and selling of political influence, and if restricting or eliminating them will purify the system, how does that stop the Charlie Keatings out there?"

Charlie managed to move over $2 million directly into the grasping hands of the inside influence peddlers without ever having to send one thin dime through a PAC!

In the heavy buying and selling taking place in Washington and other government circles, PACs are really nonentities. Since PAC money first has to be raised from individuals, it's a simple process to eliminate the PAC function by routing the individual payments directly to the seller. Surely, if the American Medical Association PAC were closed tomorrow there would be nothing to stop those dollars from moving directly from doctor to politician. Actually such direct action on the part of influence buyers would save them money by eliminating the considerable overhead of PAC administrative costs. Of course this would also eliminate a substantial group of professional buyers from the pipeline and might create an unemployment crisis in Washington!

Quite simply, as the system exists today, eliminating Political Action Committees would have no discernable effect on the buying and selling of government. Of course, knowing this, we may expect our triumphant political leaders to place some sort of glossy restriction on PACs. Call this "reform" a standoff. Although selling well in Peoria, it represents no gain or loss for either buyer or seller.

What about some of the other "reforms" being debated by the inmates? Next to PACs, nothing draws as much passion from politicians than the high total costs of election campaigns. On this subject there can be little argument over the mind-boggling prices elections are going for today. Individual campaigns for Senator or State Governor regularly top $10 million and even $20 million! Few logical points can be raised against reducing these costs. In this area there are almost as many proposed solutions as there are politicians seeking office.

Strong, if varied, support is heard for some system of government (that translates to taxpayer in realspeak) financing of major campaigns, á la the Presidential Campaign subsidy. In pure theory (if we can use the term pure for something out of Washington) this one is attractive, but in practice it presents a heavy minefield. Since the presidential races are the only ones so financed, we need look no further than those for experience on this "reform." The federal government (us) provides over $100 million to the presidential follies every four years. Proponents of this type of subsidy point with pride at this one, noting that since each candidate shares equally from the pot they are playing on a "level playing field." How can you be so crass as to argue against such equality, isn't that in the American tradition?

Our national sports of football and baseball would become mountain climbing contests if they had to endure the "level playing field" as defined by our political insiders. The previously detailed secret slush fund raised by the GOP's Mosbacher sure provided a sizable chunk of high ground for his candidate George Bush on the 1988 "level playing field"! But even this substantial promontory wasn't nearly as critical as that provided by the hundreds of state and local campaign headquarters, Republican, Democrat, and union, doing their unreported bit for their presidential nominee. There is no way anyone could ever calculate the millions in cash and campaign services shoved through the open doors in the campaign finance laws. No "reform" mentions shutting these doors.

Taxpayer financing of campaigns cannot produce the "level playing field" so passionately preached unless the unregulated landscapers are kept out of the picture. Listen carefully to the rhetoric on this "reform": You will hear little about the hidden side funds that play such a big part in winning elections. On the contrary, as we'll see, there are those in powerful positions who wish to expand the role of the political party elite (who run the hidden funds) in the whole process.

There has been a lot of whimpering from participants in the system over the high costs of certain elements in their professionally crafted election campaigns. We are told the system would become less dollar hungry if only the high cost of TV advertising and postage could be reduced. Although we are supposed to assume the total dollars in campaigns would drop in concert with proposed reduced rates for video exposure and postage stamps, past experience should warn you away from that primrose path. You can bet your next tax bill that should the insiders win this "reform" by strong-arming the TV industry and Postal Service into special cut rates, two unpleasant results would inevitably follow.

The most obvious is that rather than reducing the number of dollars they are squeezing out of the influence buyers, our greedy ones will merely increase the number of TV spots they buy and the number of junk mail pieces they send us. The next result would be that TV will have to raise their rates to other advertisers to make up the cuts, ultimately leading to increased prices to the consumer. The Postal Service would also have to raise stamp prices (again) to us ordinary users or seek a government subsidy. This "reform," true to the general pattern of other actions designed by Congress to help us, will end up costing us money without stopping the rampant buying and selling of our government.

All the debate, and little action, if any, over election "reforms" will revolve around those activities most visible to the public. Political Action Committees, Federal Campaign Financing and others on public reports will be worried to death. Don't look for anything substantive being done about those invisible areas we've discussed. As we'll see, the insiders are openly talking about expanding the scope and size of the hidden financing while the debate on cleaning house continues.

Chapter 15

If Not Reform—What?

Underlying all the dodging and procrastinating over the selling of our government is a fundamental belief on the part of our leaders that what they are doing is not wrong. As complaints increase and public opinion watchers report a universal contempt for Congress on the part of the public, Washington leaders stubbornly dig in their heels and rally round to protect their valuable turf. Top spokesmen for both political parties in Congress go to great lengths to publicly lament the "new" morality, the implication is plain that there must exist an "old" morality they much prefer.

Apparently their "old" morality sees no fault in the sleazy activities of former Congressman Jim Wright and Tony Coelho who were forced from office by proponents of the "new" morality. Obviously Republican Party leaders prefer the "old" morality of their own leaders—such as Bill Taylor, who amassed over $1 million in a few years of insider influence peddling, since he still holds his position of "honor" within the party. Many defenders of the "old" morality in addressing the actions of the infamous Keating Five (Senators Cranston, DeConcini, Glenn, McCain and Riegle) have excused them under the catchall term of constituent services. The list of those protected under the "old" morality is endless, including not only the suddenly rich, but such role models of sexual behavior as Congressman Barney Frank and Donald Lukens.

In response to rising public indignation, our Washington leaders are doing what they, by training and experience, are truly expert at, scamming their constituents. There have been flurries of activity by many committees in Congress, including the so-called "ethics" committees, to let us folks back home know they're really on top of things. Although the preaching is of a high order of piety, despite all the "ethics" investigations of their fellow congressional club members, you will need extremely sharp eyes and ears to detect even the mildest form of rebuke being levied against one of their own. Here we can witness the "old" morality in its purest form!

No better example of the defensive doctrine of the "old" morality can be found than in the publicized case of Charlie Keating. Congressional committee chairmen almost trampled each other in their haste to get public (prime-time TV) hearings assembled to vent their outrage over Charlie's swinging activities in the rotten savings and loan industry. Because Keating refuses to be a pussycat and curl up at the feet of the Washington masters, those hearings have been turned into a nightmare for the insider establishment. Like Pandora's box, their best efforts will be expended trying to reclose it!

Keating, head of the failed Lincoln Savings in California, unlike David Paul, head of the extinct CenTrust Bank in Florida, did not choose to face the firing squad blindfolded and gagged. While Paul quietly slipped from view, Keating went public and pointed out the obvious. To the embarrassment of the righteously angry congressmen leading the posse against the tall rider from the West, they were unable to hide the deep involvement of their own club members in the savings and loan corruption. Even though members of the House Banking Committee tried to keep the names of the prominent senators who cavorted in King Charlie's Court off the record, the lid of Pandora's box had been lifted too far. Since the Keating Five, and many of their associates connected with other S & L scandals were performing under the "old" morality, the angry Congressmen felt they should have immunity. Now what can they do?

The pattern is rapidly developing as masters of the coverup skillfully ply their trade. Members of Congressman Henry Gonzalez's House Banking Committee, in public hearings, are stifling any references to improper involvement by the senators and actually attacking any who have the temerity to attempt to bring it into the discussion. They are rallying all forces to convince the usually gullible public that Charlie Keating operated in a political vacuum accomplishing his nefarious deeds. The "old" morality decrees that members of the insider's club, like Caesar, could do no wrong!

Quickly learning that the fun and games of public hearings before TV cameras can be damaging when worm cans like the Keating affair are opened, you can anticipate our insiders giving little further public scrutiny to other, equally questionable, swingers in the S & L scandals. David Paul, of the failed CenTrust Bank (almost as large as Charlie's Lincoln Savings), has been allowed to fade into relative oblivion. To this date there has been no indication that Congressman Gonzalez has any stomach for bringing Mr. Paul and his friends to the public docket. This, despite the fact that he, of the gold yacht nails, was quite active in monetary support of his favorite Florida senator. That genie is one they want to keep in the bottle!

All of the protective camouflage is not being spread by Congress, however. The Administration of President Bush seems equally inclined to join the muting effort. Bush's Attorney General Richard Thornburgh had announced his office would not be investigating or prosecuting very many of the savings and loan crooks. The official White House line seemed to be that our chief law enforcement branch was "too busy" with other, presumably more important, wrongdoers. Since the Savings and Loan bailout plan, engineered by President Bush as one of his first actions after taking office, is now conceded to represent a cost to taxpayers in excess of $500 billion, the sluggish Attorney General's office has belatedly taken note of David Paul and other notables within the

S & L industry and requested another couple hundred million to chase the scoundrels. With President Bush's son Neil now receiving prominent attention for his activities in the S & L thing, Attorney General Thornburgh's position is not one to be envied.

At this point in the narrative let me say I'm tired of this "old" morality crap! From now on, let's call it what it really is, a protection of the "status quo."

The rally 'round the flag to protect the old good life reaches into every avenue of contact between our influence peddlers in government and their deep-pocketed buyers. There are other areas getting even deeper protection than those represented by the diversionary skirmish to sink Political Action Committees and the coverup for the savings and loan gang, in and out of government.

In the volumes of rhetoric over reform there seems to be no one addressing the broad subject of lobbying. With almost 25,000 known lobbyists prowling the sanctified halls of government in Washington, not to mention the closet lobbyists like Bill Taylor, you'd think the subject deserves at least casual mention in the debates. With all those thousands of individuals and organizations spending unlimited millions of dollars to buy votes in Congress, none of which comes under any meaningful regulation, you would think the reformers could at least administer a token slap on the wrist! Again, apparently under the insiders' "old" morality (status quo), the lobbyists are merely demonstrating the working of the free market in buying our government.

There have been some tentative moves towards addressing the subject of "soft" (which we call hidden) money. As is their predictable habit, when they know they have a good thing going, the approach will be certain not to present any real danger to the status quo. Already proposed by one group of senators (Republicans of course) is the abolition of "soft" money accounts such as the lucrative plaything of Democrat Senator Alan Cranston. The theme of this sermon is that private "soft" money accounts are inherently evil and must be driven from the temple. On the other hand insider "soft" money, as generated by the national political parties is "holy" money and that practice must be preserved. On this issue, especially, you can see a pattern developing on the way insiders intend to protect their access to the really big secret dollars.

By selling the idea the two national political parties are the souls of propriety in the process of selling our government, the Washington gang aim to increase the undercover money channels in the name of "reform." Public reporting of political money will be limited to listing those small, relatively inconsequential, public donations, while the really big payoffs are handled in secret. Even President George Bush, speaking, undoubtedly, from his training while National Chairman of the Republican Party, has advocated giving a larger role to the political parties in raising and distributing funds through the political system. Coinciding with this position are strong rumors circulating in Washington that commerce Secretary Robert Mosbacher is slated to become the next Chairman of the Republican Party. Who better to take over, as more emphasis is placed on "soft" money flowing through parties, than the GOP's premier producer of such hidden funds!

We headed this chapter, "If Not Reform—What?" for good reason. The "What" is an expansion of the channels through which hidden money is used to buy our government along with a simultaneous back of the hand to those channels normally open to public scrutiny. To coin a twisted metaphor, that backhand slap is calculated to create enough noise and smoke to obscure the expansion of the "old" morality and preserve the financial status quo!

Chapter 16

"New" Morality?

"The public looks at us as if we're all corrupt"—so laments Senator Warren Rudman of New Hampshire.

Senator George Mitchell of Maine responds that he sees it only as "unhealthy cynicism."

A private nationwide poll commissioned by the Democrat Party shows the public thinks that most important decisions are being made by lobbyists and other moneyed interests. The U.S. Congress ranks poorly behind in decision making.

A public opinion poll in California indicates that most citizens think that bribe taking is commonplace in government.

Washington insiders continue to complain that they are being asked to adhere to a higher standard than the ordinary citizen, whenever criticism is directed their way for their close relations with the influence buyers.

One of the usually accepted tenets of our American system is that sooner or later the electorate does the right thing for the country. Winning officeholders see a great deal of wisdom in that statement, while the losers, of course, think the voters missed the boat. It would appear, the way things are going, that both sides may have elements of truth in their assessment. Certainly our opening quotes would indicate the electorate is having strong second thoughts over what they have wrought in the voting booths.

Since the news media universally focuses only on the spectacular cases of wrongdoing, like the Keating Five, former House

Speaker Jim Wright, and former Senator Gary Hart, where does the public get the general perception that outside interests are in control of our government? The strong feeling that bribery is rampant indicates that the bad feeling for our governing elite goes beyond mere concern for undue influence over the process. Although Senator Mitchell may continue to write this off as just "unhealthy cynicism," it appears to this writer that the public is rapidly turning against all government. The senator and his exclusive club members would do well to pull their collective heads out of the morass in Washington and take a close look at what is happening in the real world.

Perceptions pertaining to an individual's quality and character usually take a long time to change. The natural instinct of the American public is to support and wish officeholders well as they tackle the task of running the country. It takes a lot of strong negatives for that good perception in the public mind to change. If they're now thinking bribery and corruption is a serious problem, you can bet it is already an epidemic! It does no good for leaders such as Senator Rudman to live in a fool's paradise thinking they have only to clear out a few bad apples. The entire clubroom is badly in need of fumigation!

Probably the biggest mistake made by the Washington elite corps is their fixed belief that most of us simply don't comprehend what has been happening. Along that line we go back to the earlier quoted position of former Mayor Daley of Chicago. You will recall his warning about the danger they engendered by letting the public see their growing affluence. Obviously no such friendly warning has ever been passed along to our ego-ridden members of Congress. It has not passed the notice of most citizens that the people they send to Washington seem to become personally wealthy in a relatively short time in that closed society. This, despite the fact that their representatives constantly bemoan their poor plight struggling to get along on the mere pittance they receive in pay. As a typical illustration, allow me to relate a case from my own personal experience in the political jungle.

Some years ago I was approached by a young man who showed a driving ambition to get into government by running for his state legislature. Counseling with him, I pointed out that the elected position he sought, while time-consuming to the incumbents, was technically a part-time job paying less than $8,000 per year salary. He assured me he was ready to give up his minor job with a large corporation and devote himself to serving the public. With no real assets beyond his aging automobile, he said his wife was ready to seek a job to help support the family on this mission of public service.

The enthusiastic candidate won his election and did devote himself full-time to doing a good job in the state legislature. After a few terms at that training level, he ran successfully for a seat in the U.S. House of Representatives. During his four subsequent terms as a representative he has done a pedestrian job, never making waves but keeping his home district constituents satisfied enough to keep sending him back. Certainly not an unusual case: there are many more in Congress just like him.

The congressman has received little personal criticism: he has not overworked the rubber chicken honoraria circuit or been too obvious on overseas junkets. Despite this, however, there is still a feeling of unease among many of his constituents that apparently also is typical of other similar congressional districts. The largely unspoken concern is over their congressman's net worth as dutifully reported by the press every year. During his relatively short tenure in Washington this representative's net worth has risen from near zero to over $4 million! Raised eyebrows on the part of his constituents should not be unexpected as he has no visible business or employment aside from his government position.

Although Senate Majority Leader George Mitchell would not agree, these things do contribute to serious cynicism over just what is happening in Washington. No one begrudges the great American dream of economic success. It's just that they would like to know why insiders in Washington seem to have the inside track.

As a sharp contrast to the majority who have become wealthy under liberal campaign finance rules, honoraria, soft money deals, and inside business connections, consider the record of Congressman William H. Natcher of Kentucky.

Representative Natcher has represented his district in the U.S. House for thirty-six years. Although that is a better than average record for longevity, it alone is not the reason William Natcher is unusual. In a body Senator Rudman says the public feels is universally corrupt, Natcher stands out like a shining beacon.

Representative Natcher, in thirty-six years of continuous service in the heady atmosphere of Washington has never accepted an honorarium for a speech! Rapidly approaching four decades of service to his constituents, he has never missed a floor vote in the House of Representatives (his votes total over 16,000). Mr. Natcher, considered by many a jewel among swine, frequently gets the opportunity to speak to incoming freshman Congressmen. To these neophytes Natcher says, "There are lots of things in life that are right, sacred, and good—and one of them is to serve in the Congress and say to those who want to spend money on you, 'I'd appreciate it if you would just keep your hands off me!' "

Although most of the influence buyers know enough to leave Congressman Natcher alone, occasionally one of them tries. The stately, seventy-nine year old representative just sends the checks back. In 1988 Natcher spent only $8,400 on his reelection campaign, most for auto expenses as he drove around his sprawling rural district. Compare that to most of the campaigns in compact urban districts where his Washington associates averaged better than $500,000 in campaign costs!

William Natcher's natural and refreshing fiscal conservatism extends to his office in Washington, which is the lowest budgeted office in the entire Congress. Eschewing the showbiz-oriented setups of his fellow Congressmen, Natcher has no administrative assistant, legislative director or press secretary. As he puts it, he just has "five ladies" in his office to help out.

Naturally, many of Representative Natcher's associates have difficulty disguising their contempt for his dogged devotion to the job he considers a sacred trust, and particularly his unparalleled honesty. He is, however, no wimp, serving as a senior member of the powerful House Appropriations Committee and frequently presiding over the House during especially difficult debates! Now, what is wrong about this story on Kentucky Congressman William Natcher?

Out of the more than 500 elected members of Congress, why does Representative Natcher stand out as so unusual? Why does unwavering honesty, a refusal to be bought by special interest money, an unwillingness to pack his staff with high-priced ego builders, and a determined devotion to performing the job he was elected for, make him unusual?

That's what is wrong with his story. With those characteristics he should be so commonplace in Washington as to be unworthy of special note! Why is it we don't expect, no, demand, that all our elected officials meet the same basic standards set by William Natcher? Why do we just sit back and lament the dishonesty and graft, why don't we call our own elected elite and tell them to see William Natcher for a general reprogramming?

Are we talking about a "new" morality here, as the majority of Washington insiders insist? Does William Natcher's story sound like "new" morality to you, or does it sound like old-fashioned values, the kind our parents and teachers taught us about when we were growing up? Is it necessary or effective to have "ethics" and campaign commissions holding a gun to the heads of our leaders to force them to behave like William Natcher? I can find nothing in the record that indicates Congressman Natcher's strength of character resulted from some muddled campaign law or politically appointed board forcing him to behave.

I've never met William Natcher, but I think I know how he would answer if asked why he does things the way he does, "Because that's the way Mom taught me!"

Sadly, Congressman Natcher will probably finish his distinguished career with nothing more than a handshake for his service. Somewhere along the way Congress will probably vote to build a marble monument or plush office building to the memory of sleazebag Jim Wright, but don't look for a memorial to William Natcher: He's a real embarrassment to those who prefer to sell out our heritage.

The precedent, unfortunately, is there, the good ol' boys built a giant Congressional office building in honor of former Congressman Sam Rayburn. Good ol' Sam used to keep the lower drawer of his desk filled with good American cash. Those favored cohorts in the hallowed halls of Congress who did good in the eyes of Sam received $2,000 to $3,000 handouts from their leader!

How can William Natcher compete with that?

Chapter 17

Physician, Heal Thyself!

Even as this is being punched into the word processor, the all-powerful insiders in Washington are beginning to sigh with relief and settle back into their regular business as usual. Satisfied that their massive efforts to sell the country on the insiders' version of campaign "reforms" has turned the tide of public opinion with no major battle damage, Washington is gradually returning to being the fun-filled capital it used to be before outsiders tried to spoil the game. That nothing of substance has been or will be changed can be readily ascertained by only a cursory examination of where they are coming from.

The elitists, and their joyful supporting chorus from the media, are smoothly moving toward what they insist are meaningful "reforms." In the forefront, it appears that PACs (Political Action Committees), .the perennial bad boys of the electoral system, will be marched to the gallows with bands playing and colors unfurled. As the gang madly cheers this ritual sacrifice, let's fall back to a neutral corner and contemplate what this major act of Congress will really accomplish.

Political Action Committees are, by definition, special interest groups formed to promote narrow interest results in government laws or actions on their behalf. As such, they do come fully under the admittedly weak and inadequate Federal Election Commission regulations. PACs must file regular reports with the FEC, detailing where and from whom they got their money, and where and on whom they spent it. This money, unlike over 90 percent of political slush funds, is a matter of public record, and any citizen is free to examine the reports and read the names. The fact that they are on public record is why the lazy media so frequently reports on their activities: It doesn't take any strenuous research on their part. The fact that these reports are so readily available is a continuing embarrassment to politicians at the top state and federal levels. Hardly is the ink dry on final election results before the news media is running sensational stories about which money-grubbing senator or representative got how much money from special interest PACs!

There can be little argument that PACs wield a pervasive influence over our government functioning. Even the least attentive citizen knows instinctively that Senator Grabalot is not going to kill many bills favorable to organized labor after labor PACs were so generous in his last campaign. As the self-righteous clamor rises to "kill the PACs," however, keep one important fact in mind: PACs are on the public record and you can always find out who gave it and who got it!

How bad really, in the overall picture, are the PACs? From the blizzard of rhetoric coming from the politicians and the media, one would believe they represent the major factor in the sellout of our government. As in all things emanating from Washington, the truth is far different from the snow-job "facts" being showered on the populace. Consider the following real truths, all from the certified public record,

> During the 1988 election year, pro-Israel PACs, numbering over thirty individual groups, gave a total of \$4.5 million to political candidates.
>
> For the year 1989, PACs representing all facets of the defense industry, certainly the largest group of recipients of federal tax dollars, contributed \$2 million to our politicians in Washington.

The list could go on, but these instances represent two of the largest special interest groups working the Washington territory.

Certainly, by most reckoning, these are not minuscule sums, but, remembering they do file public reports, consider the following:

> Charlie Keating funnelled over $2 million into the grabbing hands of our elite political leaders, and he never used a PAC!
>
> Robert Mosbacher raised and spread over $30 million into the inside government track, all without any PACs or public reports!

So, the grubby insiders tell us they're going to make their world politically pure by eliminating PACs! Just what are they going to do about the other 90 to 95 percent being slipped into the political slush pots? Well, as the late straight shooter, John Wayne would have put it, "Listen up, pilgrims!"

One proposal, presented in the laudable guise of returning elections to the "grass roots," would increase the existing limitations on individual contributions to candidates. On this "reform" the $1,000 cap that individuals can give to a single candidate and the $25,000 limit on total contributions would be increased. Now, here, we're talking real "grass roots" participation in the electoral system! I'm sure that most of you have been chafing under the law that only allows you to give $25,000 per campaign to your favorite influence peddlers! Think how this will reduce the strain on high bidders: Guys like Charlie Keating wouldn't have to find so many relatives and employees to launder his money into the system as he did under the old limit! Chalk this one up for gold-plating the "grass roots"!

But, grab your seat belts, now that the dam has been broken, it seems there will be no end to the "reforms" flowing from the asylum! Recognizing that "soft" money constitutes a problem, our Washington housecleaners are taking dead aim on that one too! All are in stern-faced agreement that private "soft" money slush funds, such as the one run by Senator Cranston & Son, must be stopped. Suddenly recognizing the dangers in these so-called "voter registration" and "get out the vote" money pots being in the hands of outsiders, our insiders are ready to mow them down at the pass!

"But wait," say some of the more studious types in the system. "Voter registration and encouragement are popular objectives, let us not kill that golden goose!" So, folks, what we're going to do in this "reform" is not a total kill of "soft" money, but redirecting it into the hands of the insiders who best know how to handle big unlisted slush funds! The Democrat and Republican National Committees will now have an unlimited license to create as many unreporting and unregulated hidden money accounts as they see fit. I know it makes you feel infinitely better knowing all those high bidders can now write as many $100,000 checks as they want without fear of detection. Oh, these funds will acquire high-sounding names like "voter education," but as long as they are secret who can say what the money is doing to your government?

Okay, so much for campaign fund "reforms," the new system, on balance, seems to guarantee the sellers of inside influence will still be getting top dollar from the willing buyers. But again, there are other areas where the sellers are becoming wealthy—are there other "reforms" on the way?

Conspicuously absent from all the high-sounding speeches and committee hearings is any sign of any real indignation toward one of Washington's major industries, lobbying. The expensive act of lobbying is closely related to the effort put forth by Political Action Committees, with one very important difference. Lobbyists can conduct their trade in almost total secrecy, while PACs must file public reports. It should come as no surprise that lobbyists in Washington easily outnumber PACs by an order of over 100 to one!

As our political friends like to say, "Let's look at the record!"

The known and unknown lobbyists roaming the Washington halls alone total at least 25,000. The avowed purpose of every lobbyist is to persuade senators, representatives and bureaucrats that their particular cause merits favorable attention ahead of and above any of the other 24,999. By the numbers alone, you know how fierce the competition for the ears and votes of Congress must be. That they spare little expense in their quest is readily noted from the many luxurious entertainment facilities they own, or patronize, inside and out of Washington. Let's get it all on the chart, so to speak, and use a conservative estimate of the annual expenditure by each lobbyist in his mission to buy favors from our elite insiders. Assume each lobbyist buyer has a budget of $10,000 per year to buy favorable votes and actions—I would say a reasonable assumption knowing that the GOP leader William Taylor so casually offered $25,000 in a single bribe!

Sit down as you read this, we're talking about over $250 million the lobbying gang is pouring into the bidding war annually for control of our government! There is no way that anyone can equate PACs, no matter how prevalent, to the conservatively estimated one quarter billion dollars coming from the uncontrolled lobbyists! PACs, however, are doomed to the guillotine while lobbyists will grow and prosper under our leaders' "reforms"!

At this point we won't even attempt to get into the subject of the plush tropical resorts, deep-sea fishing yachts, championship golf courses, and north woods hunting and fishing lodges maintained and used in secret for the care and amusement of our elite insiders courtesy of the high bidders. It would take a separate book to detail big winners like former Congressman Tony Coelho's insider junk bond profits or William Taylor's lucrative part ownership in government-funded housing projects.

But, how about the moral issues, beyond the morality of the direct monetary payoffs in the bidding wars? Despite indignant cries of "new morality," there are many other factors in the degrading of our government that cry out for corrective therapy. Even though these matters only receive pattycake treatment, if any, by the news media, judge for yourself whether they represent quality leadership by our public officeholders.

Consider, for example, the personal conflicts of Secretary of State James Baker during his career in Washington. While Presidential Chief of Staff in the White House, and later as Secretary of the Treasury, Baker owned a large block of shares in the Texas Commerce Bank. As Secretary of Treasury he exerted his considerable insider influence before Congress in support of legislation favoring interstate bank mergers. As a result of this legislation, Chemical Bank of New York took over the Texas institution and Secretary Baker ended up owning Chemical shares valued in the $3 million to $4 million range. Later, again in his official capacity as Treasury Secretary, Baker applied U.S. Government pressure to keep Brazil from stopping payment on its U.S. bank debts. Had Brazil stopped payment, Chemical Bank, holder of sizable notes from that country, would have suffered substantial losses. Baker made no public disclosure of his personal conflict of interest at the time!

When, later, as he served as Secretary of State in President Bush's Cabinet, questions were raised about him holding such large investments in banks directly affected by foreign policy decisions from his department, the Bush Administration acknowledged that this concern represented a "new standard"!

"New Standard," "New Morality," aren't we being flooded with catchall phrases to justify everything the insiders want to do?

Getting flashes of publicity, then quickly fading into obscurity, are many evidences of personal morality breakdowns at the highest government levels. The media, as well as the political insiders, are quick to brush aside any suggestion that gutter-level morals might adversely affect governing decisions, and neither group cares to discuss the issue. Removing the camouflage from these affairs helps in understanding the general deterioration endemic to Washington.

For a while, the continuing saga of Representative Barney Frank (MA) even displaced some of the truly bizarre Hollywood characters off the front pages and prime time. Frank, after some uncaring snoop forced revelation of his homosexual lifestyle, revealed that his favorite young male prostitute lived full-time with him in his Washington apartment. Apparently to make sure the romance wasn't prematurely dissolved, Congressman Frank placed the male prostitute on the payroll. Apparently this ungracious male stud was not satisfied with Barney alone, for he turned Frank's apartment into a homosexual prostitution business headquarters!

Although the personal morals of Barney Frank are such as to shock most people, even more shocking is the nearly universal support he has received from the ever so righteous Congressional leadership and the adoring Washington media. We are constantly assured by this out-of-touch society that Barney Frank is a superior congressman and that the country can ill afford to lose him; therefore, his personal behavior should be condoned in the interest of keeping him in position to make major decisions on the course of our country. Under this insider moral standard, deviant activities are considered chic. Sometimes you have to wonder whether we're dealing with the center of our government or with ancient Athens. Even more off the wall than Frank's boyfriend's officially protected business, if that's possible, is the case of Washington man about town, Craig Spence.

The *Washington Times* newspaper some time ago broke the story about Spence's swinging parties frequented regularly by Washington's top insiders. Sparing no expense at these affairs, Spence provided a choice of male prostitutes (and occasional females for those with traditional tastes) suitable for any special desires of his guests. Besides the usual heavy assortment of booze, a mandatory staple at insider affairs, Spence also saw to it that his guests had a steady supply of cocaine to liven up the proceedings. The *Times* also reported that Spence apparently made secret video tapes of his important guests and sexual professionals in action. Unfortunately, or fortunately, depending on which side of the fence you happen to be on, that newspaper seemed to bury the continuing story before they got to the damaging revelations. It does leave one speculating, however, as to what use those tapes are being put to. As some top government officials stated, off the record, they could be material for serious blackmail against top government participants!

Although the *Times* story went on to indicate the kind of clout Craig Spence had at high levels, it also died without follow-up. The story detailed how Spence conducted post-midnight tours of the White House for his friends and their male prostitutes. Implicit in the unchallenged accusation was the fact such activities could not have occurred without substantial assistance from some highly placed government leaders—probably why the story was abruptly dropped!

As of this writing there has been no official action taken on Craig Spence's White House tour service. Barney Frank, however, received a reprimand from the House of Representatives—nothing more.

Let's get serious now about what needs to be done to get our government back. It should be obvious by now that the farcical moves being proposed by Congress, along with the concerted coverups of unethical activity, simply are not going to cut the mustard. As you probably suspect by now, your indignant author does have a few suggestions to make!

Before getting to actual methods that could be effective in bringing our Congress and overall government back to the people, we must accept some basics. Since we have literally millions of pages of regulations and laws purporting to protect our interests in good government, and the blatant sellout of our heritage continues, we'll have to reluctantly concede more pages of the same aren't going to get the job done. Admitting that law has failed brings us again to the conclusion a different cure is needed.

If we quit trying to fight the questions concerning morality, and simply admit that a lack of moral fiber is at the root of all our governing problems, we are in position to institute some meaningful changes. Remember, laws prohibiting spitting on the sidewalk would have been almost impossible to enforce had not those being regulated seen the logic in those laws. The regulations became effective when the public realized spitting on the sidewalk was unhealthy and therefore unsafe. We could throw away those laws now without worrying about going back to open spitting.

High bidders controlling our government cannot be squelched until those in control accept the fact that it is not only immoral, but unhealthy. So, new laws and regulations will not do the trick, our leaders and the general public must first buy the fact that it must not be allowed to continue because of the very real threat to our future health as a nation. Here, then, is one man's suggestion for action.

Congress should close down for a sixty-day period. All federal government offices should be put on a minimum skeleton staff for the same period (this part may be quite difficult since the perpetual motion machine that is our national bureaucracy is almost impossible to adjust). All senators, representatives, White House staff, and top bureaucrats should be ordered out of Washington for that sixty days and required to go back home to the source of their roots.

Once home, a moratorium should be placed on all political meetings or contacts. During this period, all key government insiders should be required to spend at least one week staying with Mom and Dad. If the old folks are no longer with us, I'm sure Aunt Mabel and Uncle Ned would be happy to put the family senator or representative up for one week!

During this long-overdue visit, while Mom has our ego-driven insider sitting at the kitchen table, with a glass of milk and some home-made cookies, heart-to-heart family talk is warranted. Hopefully this familiar environment from long ago and long nearly forgotten will encourage our nation's leaders to open up for the kind of free exchange only possible in a loving family relationship.

Tell Mom about that expensive Rolex watch you're wearing and the luxury Mercedes you left parked in her driveway. Tell her about your good friends from the Widget Association who slipped you the generous "honoraria" that allowed you to enjoy these finer things in life. While you're entertaining Mom with these anecdotes from your life in Washington, be sure to bring out the pictures you took at that fun-filled family vacation you took in Acapulco last year. As Mom raises her eyebrows over the obvious cost of the luxuries depicted in your colorful pictures, assure her that this, too, was provided through the generosity of another good friend who represents the major government contractor for that new supersonic bomber she has seen on TV.

While you're opening up with Mom about the wonderful things you have been doing in Washington, set her mind easy about your strenuous life by pointing out how you've been able to accumulate a substantial nest egg for the future despite the meager salary you get from the taxpayers. You don't need to go into too much detail, just the basics about how you're able to squirrel enough of your campaign funds aside to fatten the old bank account. Since you might be planning on early retirement, she will be relieved to learn about the part ownership you have in that big public housing complex provided by that good developer friend in Atlanta.

Now, I don't know your mom, but I know what my mom would have done during a similar visit. She is going to ask you some questions. "But, Son, when you and your friends passed that Widget bill, prices went so high that your dad and I had to postpone getting a new Widget. You know our old one is getting so worn we can't enjoy it anymore!" and, she'll probably go on, "I don't see why we needed that funny-looking new Air Force bomber. Couldn't you have voted to spend some of that money to fix up our highway? Dad and I blew a tire last week in a big pothole on the Interstate while we were trying to see your ailing aunt in Fartown!"

I'm sure you get the picture, Senator, no doubt your mom would have equally pointed questions concerning donations towards your election that eventually went into your pocket, or the wonderful investment you acquired for nothing as a result of the Corrupt Department of Housing and Urban Development! I'm sure you found it difficult to look Mom directly in the eye and tell her you did all these things because that's "the way it is" in Washington. If your memory hasn't become too scrambled by the good life of a Washington insider, maybe you also recalled what Dad told you as a youngster, "Don't expect more than you deserve, and don't take more than you've honestly earned!"

Can you really see anything wrong with the basic value standards expressed by Mom and Dad? Has the corrupt atmosphere in Washington so muddled your brain cells that you cannot remember how you were brought up? Surely you know that those big campaign donations, stealthy honoraria, and inside investments are not pure love offerings. Surely you, who wouldn't pick up a magazine from the newsstand without paying for it, know what you're taking is just as much stealing as that?

The sixty days are up, how about going back to Washington and performing your job as though Mom were still sitting across the table from you?

Being an incurable optimist, I'm sure that such a return to our roots by our leaders would do wonders for the future of our country. I can see a real pride of accomplishment on the part of our Congress as they approach their jobs carrying some of the old fashioned values from home. I can see enthusiasm on the part of the constituents back home as their elected representatives become real people instead of the hyped up super egos they've watched in recent years. Wouldn't it be great if they did come back renewed, refreshed, and chafing at the bit to get cracking on saving the Union?

Let's fantasize over what might happen after such a homecoming.

Forget about all the "reform" plans, let's look at removing or replacing the problem rules and starting anew. Abolish PACs entirely, prohibit all "soft" (secret) political funds entirely, regardless of source. Limit political parties to their original mission, providing old fashioned volunteer help in election campaigns. Restrict all campaign donations to citizens of the district or state voting for the political office. Limit donations to some reasonable limit such as $100 per real person.

Further, ban all mailing from their Washington offices by incumbents for six months prior to elections. Require all political mailing be paid at the same postal rate we pay when we write a letter to the kids in Cleveland. Require all candidates spend at least 50 percent of their campaign time at unpaid appearances within their election district. Make it mandatory that at least six of their public appearances be made jointly with all other candidates for the same office. Require all public advertisements directly quote the candidate (print) or be performed by the candidate (TV and radio).

Now that wasn't difficult was it? We don't need 500 pages of another act of Congress to do what needs to be done. Such real changes, not cosmetic "reforms," would go a long way toward bringing elections back to the "grass roots" our leaders like to talk about so frequently. This suggestion, and others to follow, are freely offered for use by any senator or representative with the courage to put them to active debate on the floors of Congress!

While we're on a roll, let's agree that honoraria are out. Henceforth all public appearances, when the guest feels they are not interfering with important work in Washington or back home, will be made at no charge to the hosts. Actual travel expenses would be allowed, but not by unaccounted for lump cash payments. Most government agencies have quite comprehensive travel expense forms that their employees must use, and there's no reason why our leaders couldn't use the same to justify travel charges to these meetings.

Cut out all the "free" vacations. This is a tougher area, since we've long had laws requiring that such gifts be explicitly reported by dollar value. Since that requirement has been so openly violated over the years, it is probably naive to think things will change. Suppose we just remind the gang of how Mom would feel about these freebies; that should help clean it up!

Now we are approaching the area that really excites this old writer! The positive effects here are really mind boggling.

First, some 25,000 people would lose their reason for being in Washington and would probably leave to seek honest work elsewhere! Such unemployment would not have much negative effect on our overall economy; since most of these lobbyists are skillful enough to find productive jobs anywhere in the country. Putting all that ability back into honest labor would quickly create a positive impact on the nation's gross national product!

Another real benefit from the elimination of this, one of the world's oldest professions (note, I didn't say oldest), would accrue to all of us ordinary citizens. Washington's hotels, restaurants and limited parking spaces would suddenly become more accessible to ordinary people. Since Washington is, by far, the most popular place in the country to visit, more of our children could get to see the heart of our nation. Restaurants and hotels would quickly make up the lost lobbyists' business with greatly increased tourist trade. Oh, maybe they'd have to cut back some of their more exotic amenities to something more affordable, but they know how to make reasonable profits that way too. Think of the pleasure they would all have watching youngsters and young families enjoying their national heritage; business in Washington could be fun again!

Let's not forget the bonus we'd enjoy in the increased efficiency of our governing process. Senators and representatives would no longer have to break away early from their legislative tasks to meet the anxious lobbyists on hot golf courses or unhealthy smoky lounges. Comfortable in their clean, healthily air-conditioned work places, minds unmuddled by the constant routine of lobbyist cocktail luncheons, there is little doubt our congressional gang could give us renewed leadership.

Maybe, and this is something to be fervently hoped, with the lobbyists no longer crowding the scene, our elected leaders will have enough time to visit with their real constituents. I suspect this is part of what "government for the people" really meant when the founding fathers coined the phrase!

None of these things would be really hard to accomplish. All that our chosen leaders need to do is tack the following up on their office walls, "I'm not going to accept anything I haven't honestly earned by doing the job I was elected to do."

Why should it be so hard to tell the big bidders that our government is not for sale? Maybe it will take a while to get accustomed to normal family vacations back home among real friends, instead of on a tropical island or ocean yacht. I bet they'd all find it's just as easy to tell time with a Timex as with a Rolex, and a good old Chevy can get from here to there just as readily as a Rolls!

Think of all the positive things you'll begin to notice in place of those polls calling you crooks. See how good the old home town looks compared to the ratty whirl of Washington. Pay particular notice of how sincere your old friends back home are when they say "good morning" or "good to see you," compared to the phony back-slappers you've been enduring in the bidding wars.

I happen to believe in the innate goodness of the American spirit. I firmly believe that things can be turned around and we can get our government back. How about it, gang, why don't we give it a try?